*Pupil Personnel Services*

# The Library of Education

A Project of The Center for Applied Research in Education, Inc.
G. R. Gottschalk, Director

*Categories of Coverage*

|  I  |  II  |  III  |
| :---: | :---: | :---: |
| Curriculum and Teaching | Administration, Organization, and Finance | Psychology |

|  IV  |  V  |  VI  |
| :---: | :---: | :---: |
| History, Philosophy, and Social Foundations | Professional Skills | Educational Institutions |

# Pupil Personnel Services

**DONALD G. FERGUSON**

*Associate Professor, Special Education*
*Kent State University*

1963
The Center for Applied Research in Education, Inc.
*Washington, D.C.*

LIBRARY OF CONGRESS
CATALOG CARD NO.: 63-8459

PRINTED IN THE UNITED STATES OF AMERICA
C 7060

# *Foreword*

The time has arrived when it is necessary to clarify and to relate properly the various pupil personnel services which have come to be recognized as important and integral parts of the American educational enterprise. Educators and laymen alike have sometimes questioned the purposes to be served by the various specialists who are identified with these services. The specialists themselves have, upon occasion, accused each other of overlapping functions, of usurping responsibilities, and of independent action. With larger and larger school systems serving ever-increasing numbers of students, the need for a coordinated system of services designed to help each pupil develop and maintain his individuality in a complex of mass education experiences is a practical necessity. To serve the function which is uniquely theirs, these services must at the same time derive from the same philosophical base as other aspects of American educational policy and practice.

Donald G. Ferguson is unusually well qualified for the authorship of this monograph. He has served as a classroom teacher and school psychologist for elementary and secondary schools. He is affiliated with the Ohio State Department of Education as a supervisor of school psychological services in the Division of Special Education and is actively engaged in the preparation of pupil personnel specialists at Kent State University. He has performed a distinct service to the profession in the preparation of this publication. It will be useful for in-service work with teachers and other staff members, and as a reference for teachers, counselors, and other educators in training; it will provide a valuable source of information for school board members and others who seek a better understanding of these important services. It is a significant monograph which should enjoy wide acceptance.

WALTER F. JOHNSON

Professor and Chairman,
  Guidance & Personnel Services
Michigan State University

# Contents

*Pupil Personnel Services*

# CHAPTER I

# Overview of Pupil Personnel

About fifty million children attend American elementary and secondary schools. Each of these children is a unique individual and requires that those who teach him in school and who plan his school experiences understand him as an individual. Most of these children differ only slightly from one another in mental ability, interest, and needs; but others—approximately 15 per cent of the total—differ markedly. Who identifies these differences—be they subtle or vast—and helps teachers and school administrators to plan for them? Who keeps records of the children in the district to insure that all children who are eligible to attend school are located and that their parents are informed of their obligation to see to their child's attendance? Who finds solutions to the often difficult transportation problems and insures the attendance of children who must come some distance to school and those who might be unable to make it on foot because of some physical disability? Who in the school program works with junior and senior high school pupils to help them plan their school programs and their careers? These and many other questions underlie the newest aspects of American elementary and secondary schools: pupil personnel services. Such questions are typically raised of the specialist in pupil personnel—school counselors, school psychologists, school social workers, child accounting and attendance workers, and specialists of the school health staff. These specialists, most authorities agree, are the minimum staff necessary to perform the basic services of pupil personnel. Not all school districts employ each type; teachers and administrators continue to share much of the burden for answering and solving these pupil personnel questions. But these five specialists are appearing in increasing numbers in American schools.

During the last several decades, with the addition of psychologists, counselors, social workers, and other pupil personnel specialists to the school staff, new services have been provided and new ways of attending to old services have been found. The advent of modern

1

pupil personnel work in the schools has not meant a revolutionary change for teachers or for parents. Its appearance, however, has pointed out the need for teachers, parents, and those in the community concerned with the development and welfare of children to learn more about these services and the specialists who perform them so that they can be used to the best advantage for all.

Since pupil personnel services often differ from community to community, the public in general and even members of the professional school team often have difficulty understanding clearly their purpose and scope. Parents of today's school children grew up themselves in our nation's schools during a period when testing programs, guidance counseling, school psychological services, and other pupil personnel services were found only in large metropolitan systems or in small, but wealthy, school districts. Today parents learn about these programs and specialists through the contacts their children have with the specialists in school.

A mother and father of a boy in the ninth grade receive a note from school inviting them to attend a meeting with their son's counselor. They do not know how to interpret this invitation for there was no school counselor when they went to school. Then parents were invited to come to school only to be told of their child's bad behavior or poor schoolwork or some other problem. To their surprise, however, the interview with the counselor proves to be an interesting and worthwhile invitation to join with the school in mapping out a program for their child. They find that their child too has been drawn into the planning. The school's records of the child's achievement, ability, personal and occupational interests, and many other facets of his development are spread out, and the parents and the child are helped to evaluate them in terms of courses to be taken for the coming school year and also more distant questions of college and occupational choice.

Parents are not the only ones who have difficulties in understanding the pupil personnel roles and how specialists can effectively be used in the school setting. Even some school superintendents are thus perplexed. They have heard about guidance programs and the work of the school counselor, particularly since these services have been receiving attention from the federal government through the National Defense Education Act. In some school districts superintendents are experiencing pressures from the public to employ these personnel workers. State departments of education in many instances make known that they will help to pay for such specialists. The superintendent knows he needs these personnel and wants to add them to the school staff, but he is uncertain just how to utilize them and make them fit into the overall school picture.

Teachers, as well, are informed that these specialists can help to make their work more effective and to relieve them of some of their nonteaching duties; but, lacking in actual experience, they are uncertain as to exactly what these specialists are prepared to contribute.

In some school districts where pupil personnel programs are not thoroughly clarified, teachers—like administrators—have difficulty knowing which of the specialists to call and how to arrange for their help when confronted with a problem. Does a teacher make an informal statement to the central office and wait for a specialist to call upon him, or does he refer the case to the school psychologist through a form provided from the central office? Does he go for help with children who have problems to the school psychologist or to the school social worker? How does the teacher request special testing? The teacher must be helped to know not only how the services operate but also how they can be utilized.

Typically the pupil personnel specialists—except junior and senior high school counselors—operate out of the central office in the school district rather than being a regular part of the staff of the individual school. In most school systems the specialists often are called upon to serve the needs of many schools.

The size of the district, its finances and past history of special services, community needs, and administrative attitudes are all factors that determine the framework in which pupil personnel services operate. These will differ from district to district. In order to understand clearly how these services operate, it is essential to know something first about the overall community circumstances and about the general administrative and instructional framework of the schools. Some patterns and responsibilities exist which are common to all districts; and, while there is often overlap in services that the several specialists perform, each has special training and competencies and each does provide certain unique services.

# CHAPTER II

# Definition and Basic Principles

The pupil personnel program is composed of a group of services and functions in elementary and secondary schools which aim to adapt the school program to the needs of the learner and to help the learner adjust to the school program. They are essentially services which assist teachers and administrators in carrying out their responsibilities and are often provided directly to the learner.

The activities which fall within the scope of pupil personnel work are varied; and although carried out by all members of the school staff, they are central responsibilities of several specialists: the school counselor, school psychologists, school social worker, medical and health specialists, and child accounting and attendance workers. Only occasionally are all of these specialists found in an organized and well-coordinated department of pupil personnel. On the other hand, all school districts provide some of these services.

Counseling services, which are among the most rapidly expanding aspects of the pupil personnel program, exist at present mainly in the secondary schools. Their purpose is to guide students in educational and vocational planning. Counselors most frequently work directly with students aiding them in selecting courses, choosing an appropriate vocation, and in deciding upon and making application to a college or university. Counselors also help students to resolve some of their personal social conflicts, particularly as these occur during the hectic years of adolescence.

Psychological services have as their primary function the study of pupils who for one reason or another appear not to be profiting adequately from the school program. The school psychologist works closely with teachers and school administrators in arranging special programs for children who have learning difficulties, behavioral difficulties, and for those who—as a result of some physical disability—need specific attention.

In a typical community, approximately 17 out of each 1,000 school pupils have impaired vision or imperfect hearing and require special instructional arrangement. With such children expert diagnosis and planning must precede decisions on class placement.

Social work services, like those of school psychology, have as their primary concern the study of pupils who are not benefitting from their experience in school. The services of the school social worker are usually brought to bear on problems which require working closely with parents and often involve calling upon community agencies for help in diagnosis and treatment.

School health services, one of the older aspects of pupil personnel services, originally appeared as part of the broader community effort to control communicable diseases. Although still maintaining this responsibility, school health services have shifted in emphasis toward helping to insure that all school children are in optimum condition to profit from the school program. Where formerly nursing services were provided to the schools by a public health nurse attached to the county health office, the present trend is for schools to employ a variety of medical specialists trained in diagnostic and remedial work with school children. Modern school health programs also include a mental health effort designed to help school children learn more about good health principles.

The oldest of the pupil personnel services are those of child accounting and attendance. These services have two major responsibilities: preparing records of the whereabouts of children in the district who are eligible to attend school, and investigating and remedying problems of nonattendance. These are pupil personnel activities which are carried out in all school districts throughout the nation and which are generally provided for in compulsory school attendance legislation. Attendance services in particular have undergone a great deal of change during the past several decades. There has been a growing tendency to view nonattendance not exclusively as a discipline problem, but as symptomatic of more fundamental difficulties. Trained attendance officers now exercise their legal authority only in rare instances; more commonly they investigate cases of nonattendance in an attempt to uncover and correct the more basic problem.

These five core services are regarded by most authorities as constituting the essential services of pupil personnel.[1] However, through

---

[1] Hyrum M. Smith, "Pupil Personnel Services—What and How," *School Life,* Vol. 43 (1961), 16–18.

the years most definitions and descriptions of pupil personnel have come from authorities who represent only one of the specific services and have tended therefore to reflect a particular aspect of pupil personnel.

One of the earliest authorities to set forth a definition of these services was Arch O. Heck, who appears also to have been the first person to devote an entire text to the topic of pupil personnel. Heck defined the field as "those services whereby all children of school age are 'kept track of,' caused to attend school, and so studied that they are aided in making the maximum good use of the abilities which they have." [2]

Even today Heck's definition remains a clear and comprehensive statement of the field. It points out three major aspects of pupil personnel work: locating the children who should be in school, seeing that they get to school, and keeping them there under optimum conditions to profit from a school experience. It does reflect, however, a predominating interest in the enforcement of school attendance and the administration of the census program. These Heck identified as the "quantitative" aspects of pupil personnel work. He points only briefly to the "qualitative" aspects of pupil personnel work which are provided more directly to pupils and teachers and which are primarily concerned with insuring a positive school experience for each child.

Most prolific of the writers from the special fields have been those from guidance and counseling who often formulate definitions in terms of services to the learner. Typical of these is one provided by Strang:

> Personnel work is a fundamental aspect of education that focuses its attention on helping every individual to develop the best in him as an individual and as a member of groups. It is a process of helping persons to understand themselves by discovering their own needs, interests, and capacities; to formulate their own goals and to make plans for realizing them; and to evaluate their progress with reference, not only to self-realization, but also to potential contribution to the welfare of society.[3]

---

[2] Arch O. Heck, *Administration of Pupil Personnel* (New York: Ginn and Company, 1929), p. 12.

[3] Ruth Strang, *The Role of the Teacher in Personnel Work* (New York: Bureau of Publications, Teachers College, Columbia University, 1946), pp. 28–29.

Another frame of reference from which definitions have derived is that of school administration. The more comprehensive view of such services held by administrators is demonstrated by the definition of William A. Yeager:

> Pupil personnel administration may be defined as the provision for all those services and activities pertaining to the welfare of childhood and youth, within both the school and the community, to the immediate end that the abilities, interests, and needs of each child are increasingly realized and his greater development and good achieved, and to the ultimate end that he can become a happy, useful, contributing member of ever larger social groups.[4]

## Basic Principles Underlying Pupil Personnel Work

Despite a certain amount of overlap, the three major aspects of the American elementary and secondary school program—administration, instruction, pupil personnel service—are becoming increasingly more precise and clear-cut. One does not need to travel very far back into history to find the one-room school where the teacher alone performed virtually all of these functions of education. Specialization began with the employment of the second teacher. At that point it became necessary to assign specific responsibilities to each. As growth continued and as the school began taking on additional responsibilities, a higher degree of organization and division of labor was required.

The development of pupil personnel services is a phenomenon of the twentieth century. Since 1900, while basic functions have remained essentially the same, differences in emphasis have occurred, and new services with specialists to carry out pupil personnel functions have become increasingly common.

There is currently less emphasis on the enforcement of the attendance laws and much more on providing for conditions which will allow optimum pupil development to take place. Today, of the five major services, only child accounting and attendance have as their primary function insuring that the children are in school and attending regularly. The others work directly with teachers, school administrators, and pupils to insure that the school program is geared to the needs and abilities of pupils.

---

[4] William A. Yeager, *Administration and the Pupil* (New York: Harper & Row, Publishers, 1949), p. 26.

As the pupil personnel concept and services develop, several rather clear principles emerge.

*Pupil personnel: specialized training.* Pupil personnel work is in large measure performed by individuals who have had special training and experience in social work, psychology, or counseling, and in the applications of these disciplines to problems in the school.

A shortage of trained specialists currently exists in every phase of pupil personnel work. The typical school is apt to employ one or two specialists who perform in several areas of specialization. It is not uncommon, for example, to find the school psychologist perform social work services and have responsibilities in the guidance program. Neither is it strange to find the school counselor working also as an attendance officer. The principle on which pupil personnel is based, however, requires special competencies and skills. With time and an increase in the number of competent workers in the various specializations of pupil personnel, more departments will develop with higher degrees of specialization.

*Essentially facilitative.* While the majority of the activities of pupil personnel aim to make the teachers's job easier and more effective, they also help school administrators and at times directly serve the pupils. Their contributions in accomplishing the school's objectives are usually more indirect than direct. As McDaniel notes in discussing guidance services, ". . . they do not themselves undertake to carry out the objectives of educational programs but rather provide aids to the pupil, the teacher, and the administrator which are intended to facilitate the development of the pupil and the success of the teacher's work with him." [5]

Although the classroom teacher works directly to guide children toward desirable behavior and learning, he cannot do this effectively without the help of others, such as the school principal and the pupil personnel specialists. He relies heavily upon them to identify and select the children who should be in his class and to insure their attendance. The teacher's task is exceedingly difficult if children come to school irregularly, for the majority of his work is with groups of children and the program would lack consistency and continuity if the groups varied from day to day. Also, teachers are constantly faced with children who present learning problems

---

[5] Henry B. McDaniel, *Guidance in the Modern School* (New York: Holt, Rinehart & Winston, Inc., 1956), p. 30.

of one sort or another which lessen their ability to profit from the school program. In these instances, pupil personnel services seek to determine why children have these difficulties and what can be done about them so that proper learning can be restored.

In other instances teachers need help in the study of certain children so that they may determine whether the level and pace of instruction is appropriate. A child with some physical disability, for instance, may require special class placement. Usually handicapped children are first identified by the teacher in the regular class, and it is he who calls for evaluation to determine whether or not they are able to profit in his class. Such a case, upon referral from the teacher, requires an extensive study by pupil personnel workers in order to determine where the child might best be placed.

Although a number of pupil personnel functions are performed in part or occasionally by the teacher, personnel workers can facilitate his work through formal or informal conferences designed to help him develop necessary skills to perform these duties more effectively. This activity is usually called in-service education or staff development. The topics discussed often relate to evaluating children for purposes of promotion or retention, interviewing parents, studying children to determine matters of grouping, or simply identifying appropriate instructional levels. Although authorities generally believe that a teacher should be relieved of some of these nonteaching responsibilities, relieving him of some of those mentioned above would make his job less meaningful and make it more difficult for him to develop a warm, friendly relationship with his pupils. It is not reasonable, though, to expect him to develop any high degree of skill in these rather technical areas. He needs specialized help when situations call for a degree of competence beyond his, and he must learn how to get the necessary aid.

Pupil personnel services also facilitate the work of school administrators. The superintendent relies upon the facts and predictions of pupil personnel in order to anticipate and provide for the school's need for building expansion, for increases in teacher personnel, and for equipment and supplies. Also, he relies heavily upon pupil information supplied by personnel workers when he reports to the board of education concerning matters of increasing and decreasing school enrollments and for many of his necessary reports to the state.

Personnel specialists cooperate with administrators and supervisors in the area of curriculum to evaluate the school's instructional program through the use of standardized tests. In many school systems the standardized testing program is a function of pupil personnel. In this way curriculum planning is facilitated by the maintenance of a constant check on pupil achievement and on the relationship between the ability of children to achieve and their actual performance. Similarly, such tests are used periodically to check specific strengths and weaknesses in the school curriculum.

A third major effort of pupil personnel in furthering the accomplishment of the school's aims occurs through direct services to learners and—in some instances—parents. The school counselor, for example, spends a considerable portion of his time working with individual pupils in counseling sessions—helping them to identify, clarify, and understand feelings and attitudes which stand in the way of optimum school progress. Many students have difficulty concentrating in class because of negative feelings and attitudes which prevent them from fully applying their higher mental processes. The counselor helps both the pupil and the teacher by helping students to rid themselves of these blocks to learning. Counselors work regularly with secondary school pupils, attempting to help them make wise decisions concerning occupations and further education. One of the most important objectives of American education programs is that of self-realization for each student. This objective points out that within each pupil there is great potential for fruitful, productive, and healthful living. It makes explicit the school's intention to help each child develop in such a way as to realize his potential fully. Pupil self-realization cannot be accomplished entirely through classroom activities and is greatly aided through counseling services.

Similarly, counselors will spend time with pupils who have not been able to achieve well in school work. It is not uncommon for a pupil to be proceeding satisfactorily in the school program as measured by grades and classroom performance, yet be unable to integrate the learnings and the skills into any kind of useful and satisfying approach to real, everyday problems. Often, through a series of counseling sessions, such a pupil is brought to see more clearly the relationship between the activities of the school program and a richer and fuller life at present and in the future.

Occasionally pupil personnel workers perform a direct service for parents. The school social worker may confer with parents of a mentally retarded child, for instance, to help them gain a better understanding of the difficulties that they face in raising their child. In instances of this sort, the school social worker frequently conducts a limited number of parent interviews designed to bring about "case work readiness." Once this is established, the parents can be helped to contact a community agency which is better equipped than the school to handle a problem requiring long-term treatment.

*Developmental and problem-centered.* Over the years some of the major contribution of personnel work specialists has been helping teachers and those who plan the school program to keep in mind the developmental needs of the pupils. Illustrative are their efforts in establishing group testing programs. School systems with well-organized group testing programs appraise the learning ability and the achievement of pupils at a number of check points from kindergarten through twelfth grade. Numerous tests are used as measures of the kinds of ability and aptitude necessary to accomplish the work at different grade levels. For example, in late kindergarten or early first grade, a reading readiness test is administered to all children. This test provides the first grade teacher with information on each youngster indicating whether or not the child is ready to begin formal reading instruction or whether a continuation of the readiness program is desirable. The first grade teacher can use this information—along with other information which he has obtained during the first several weeks of first grade—as a basis for grouping. Often teachers find an advantage in being able to confer with one of the pupil personnel specialists—usually the school psychologist —to clarify some aspect of the test results which may give direction to his instructional efforts.

The group testing program continues to help identify and clarify the developmental needs of pupils throughout the range of grades. Aptitude tests, interest inventories, and school ability tests are used in the eighth and ninth grades in helping students learn more about themselves as a basis for course and career selections.

Through consultation with committees on curriculum revision, pupil personnel specialists contribute to the effectiveness of the overall school program. Committees of teachers and principals are finding these specialists of direct help in applying a knowledge of learning theory to curriculum revision, in clarifying questions of how to provide for individual differences, and in recommending measurement devices and techniques which can be used to evaluate the effects of the revised curriculum.

Of equal importance are the many problem-centered responsibilities which personnel work specialists discharge in their daily activities. Certain of the specialists, notably the school psychologists and the school social workers, spend at least half their time in the identification, diagnosis and treatment of pupil difficulties. Much of the work of the school counselor involves helping students with learning and personal problems. Often a primary grade youngster may have difficulty making the transition from home into his first large group experience. Such difficulties can usually be handled very effectively by a sensitive classroom teacher; however, at times some fairly deep seated problem of insecurity and fear arises which requires the attention of a specialist. With equal frequency senior high school students need help in handling difficulties growing out of relationships with their peers and with their parents and teachers and other authority figures.

Much of the work of pupil personnel is aimed at preventing problems, but not all problems can be prevented. Even with the best teachers, the finest school programs, and the most favorable of circumstances, there will continue to be pupil needs which make special services a prerequisite of any good school system.

*Concerned with all children.* Many of the pupil personnel services were originally brought into the school to provide for problem children. The emphasis now has changed: pupil personnel now serve all children, not just special cases.

The pupil evaluation program, for example, not only identifies the child who might be a potential problem but also provides data for planning a realistic first grade program for all children. The counseling program of the secondary school is available not just to students who have special needs but also to those who for one reason or another simply want an opportunity to talk to a friendly, accepting person about some of their concerns.

*Full use of all available resources.* Pupil personnel workers cannot work in isolation. In order to be effective, they must work in close cooperation with other school personnel and with specialists from community, regional, and state agencies. There are three types of resources which all pupil personnel specialists will regularly utilize: other pupil personnel staff members, teachers and administrators, and nonschool resources.

A great deal of personnel work is carried out on team basis. The specialists are often involved in the investigation of cases where children who are having difficulty require the attention of more than one of the specialists. Consider the case of a child referred for placement in a class for educable mentally-retarded children. The decision regarding such placement is a very weighty one involving the judgment of many people. The school psychologist, the school social worker, and the school health specialists all have a role to play in studying various aspects of the case. The director of pupil personnel is the one who will recommend for or against the placement, but in formulating his decision he will rely on the resources of his full staff.

Teachers and administrators must also be drawn into the study, for they are certainly involved in the decision. The special class teacher too can contribute meaningful insights.

In many instances a child who is the subject of a case study will be interviewed by one or a variety of community agencies, such as child guidance clinics or family service associations. Or, he might be a participant in the program of an organization such as the YMCA, Catholic Youth Organization, B'nai B'rith, or others. Any of these community agencies is in a position to contribute to the school's understanding of the child and very possibly can aid in the treatment of his problem. Often, they can participate in treatment which is beyond the scope of the school either because of the length of time required for counseling or therapy or because of the peculiar nature of the problem. There are instances, for example, when a child's problem is a preoccupation with difficulties at home which make it impossible for him to concentrate on his classroom activities. One could question whether problems of this sort are the school's responsibility, yet these unquestionably have an effect upon the child's ability to accomplish his school work. An agency such as the Family Service Association or perhaps the local clergyman can be brought into the case as a source of counseling service to help the parents to solve their problems and, consequently, alleviate those of the child and of the school.

# CHAPTER III

# Basis of Pupil Personnel Work
# and Its Historical Background

Pupil personnel services have become an integral part of the American educational system, and their validity derives from the purposes and aims of American education. These aims are individualistic and humanitarian, and in order for them to be meaningful, they must be translated into programs that will result in behavioral changes in pupils. In a very real sense, what takes place in the learner is the true measure of the effectiveness of education.

## The Aims of American Education

American elementary and secondary schools aim to produce educated people. There have been many attempts to define an educated person, and in so doing to define the aims of education. Perhaps the finest such definition is that of the Educational Policies Commission of the National Education Association which appeared in 1938, naming four broad objectives of education: self-realization, human relationship, civic responsibility, and economic efficiency.[1]

To be more meaningful and useful in providing direction for the school program, these have been translated into specific behaviors that can be identified and measured. The authors of the NEA statement have provided a lengthy list of these behaviors to enable classroom teachers to understand more clearly how to bring them about through classroom plans and activities.

The classroom teacher is the most important member of the school staff. It is he who works continuously and directly with the learner. The teacher, however, cannot perform with optimum ef-

---

[1] Educational Policies Commission of the National Education Association and the American Association of School Administrators, *The Purposes of Education in American Democracy* (Washington, D.C.: National Education Association, 1938), pp. 50, 72, 90, 108.

fectiveness without help from others, such as the principal, instruction supervisors, and pupil personnel specialists. This is particularly true now that the school is concerned not only with the academic adjustment of pupils but also with their physical, emotional, and social well-being. Staff personnel are needed who possess special competence in understanding human growth and development and in the measurement of human behavior. It is necessary for the school to identify, diagnose, and make recommendations concerning children who are not adequately profiting in the school program. These tasks, in a large measure, are the heritage of pupil personnel which is ". . . designed to create those conditions in which each individual may obtain maximum benefits from the instructional program." [2]

### Traditions and Developments

Pupil personnel is still in its infancy. One area, that of child accounting and attendance, dates back to the middle of the nineteenth century. Although there were early compulsory education laws (the earliest was enacted in Massachusetts in 1642), these were lacking in provision for compelling attendance at school. Similarly, there were no specifications concerning the ages of attendance or the time requirements within which the schools would operate. The first legislation setting forth these requirements was enacted in 1852, and again it was Massachusetts that led the way. Vermont followed shortly with the enactment of a compulsory school attendance law in 1867; and by 1929, all of the fifty states had enacted compulsory school attendance laws.[3] These laws have had a most profound effect upon the development of pupil personnel services; actually they mark its beginning. Child accounting and attendance services became necessary as state laws made local school districts responsible for keeping track of school age children and insuring their attendance.

A legalistic and accounting emphasis dominated pupil personnel

---

[2] Council of Chief State School Officers, *Responsibilities of State Departments of Education for Pupil Personnel Services* (Washington, D.C.: Council of Chief State School Officers, 1960), p. v.

[3] Nelda Umbeck, *State Legislation on School Attendance and Related Matters— School Census and Child Labor*, U.S. Department of Health, Education, and Welfare Circular No. 573 (Washington, D.C.: U.S. Office of Education, January 1, 1959), p. 13.

during the first fifty years of its history. The accounting and attendance workers were concerned with finding out which children should be in school; what children were enrolled but not attending regularly; and why certain enrolled children were not attending. These questions still underlie the functions of the attendance services of pupil personnel. Since about 1900, however, pupil personnel has been moving toward an emphasis on service to the pupil and has come to view matters of nonattendance as symptoms rather than problems.

## Development of the Newer Services

The beginning of school psychology is credited to two sources: the establishment of a Department of Child Study in the Chicago Public Schools late in the 1890's, and Lightner Whitmer, at the University of Pennsylvania, who undertook to tutor a boy who was having difficulty in school. As a result of his activities, Whitmer [4] in 1907 predicted the emergence of school psychology, claiming that a new kind of specialist who had a strong background in psychology would need to be trained to work with problem cases in the school setting.

Guidance, like school psychology, had its birth at the turn of the century. In Boston, Frank Parsons first coined the term "vocational guidance." He believed that wise vocational choices could be made only through an integration of facts concerning the world of work and the pupil; and in an effort to promote his point of view, he wrote *Choosing a Vocation* [5] in which he discussed at length the process of vocational guidance. In 1908 he founded the Vocational Bureau of Boston. Although it was located at the Civic Service House of North Boston and not in the schools, it is commonly regarded as America's first school vocational guidance program. At that early date little was known in the field of psychology of individual differences, individual measurements, or tests of vocational aptitude, ability, and interest. Consequently, Parsons' attention and that of his co-workers were devoted to studies of occupations

---

[4] R. A. Brotemarkle, ed., *Clinical Psychology: Studies in Honor of Lightner Whitmer to Commemorate the Thirty-fifth Anniversary of the Founding of the First Psychological Clinic* (Philadelphia: University of Pennsylvania Press, 1931), p. 349.

[5] Frank Parsons, *Choosing a Vocation* (Boston: Houghton Mifflin Co., 1909).

which were used to provide youth with occupational information.[6]

Meanwhile, major developments were taking place in school psychology. In 1907, the Rochester Public Schools developed a child study department and were followed in 1911 by the Cincinnati school system. The Connecticut State Board of Education in 1915 appointed a school psychologist (Arnold Gesell) to conduct psychological examinations of mentally retarded and defective children in school districts throughout the state.

School social work had its roots in the visiting teacher movement which began during the first decade of the twentieth century. It came about as part of the schools' attempt to implement the child-centered philosophy of education and as a result of the mental hygiene movement which at that time was influencing many segments of American society. Changes in philosophy of school attendance also had an influence on this field. The first school social work programs began in 1906 and 1907 in Boston, New York, and Hartford. In each of these cities the work was started by a nonschool agency that recognized the need for closer and more effective liaison with the schools and the home. Two settlement houses in New York— Greenwich House and Hartley House—assigned home visitors to work with teachers of children who were coming into the settlements. It was not until 1913 that the New York City Board of Education officially took responsibility for the program. In Boston even more credit is due to nonschool agencies for the early developments in school social work.

School health services too were emerging at the turn of the century. In 1899 Connecticut enacted laws requiring the testing of eyesight in all its public schools. At about the same time Cleveland established a dental checking program for school children. In 1902, New York began the nation's first municipally supported school nursing service.[7] And in 1911 the Joint Committee on Health Problems in Education of the National Education Association and American Medical Association was established.

During the next twenty years school health services were dominated by a concern for the prevention and control of communicable

---

6 John M. Brewer, *History of Vocational Guidance* (New York: Harper & Row, Publishers, 1942), pp. 53–64.

7 Charles C. Wilson, ed., *School Health Services* (Washington, D.C.: National Education Association, 1953), pp. 5–6.

diseases. The school, having contact with most families in the community, usually was called upon to administer a program of quarantine whenever scarlet fever, smallpox, and other diseases were diagnosed.

The second decade of the twentieth century brought many developments of historical significance in guidance and psychology. Organizations of deans of women and deans of men were established in 1914 and 1919 respectively. The testing movement originated with the first widely accepted Stanford revision of the Binet Intelligence Scale in 1916. The later development of the Army General Classification Test is of particular significance because it marked the first fruitful effort to measure intelligence on a group basis and established the group testing movement, which is now so vital to the modern guidance program. Through developments which occurred during this particular period, techniques and methods for implementing the second phase of Parsons' ideas were formulated. With the appearance of instruments to measure intelligence and other aspects of human behavior—interests, achievement, aptitudes—school counselors were able to work with pupils more effectively, helping them to achieve insights and perceptions upon which to make wise educational and vocational decisions.

Educational guidance, with its purpose of helping pupils select high school courses, also began in this second decade of the twentieth century. This different approach to guidance was first noted by Truman L. Kelley, who in 1914 published his doctoral dissertation, *Educational Guidance*.[8]

The revision of the Binet-Simon test by Louis M. Terman in 1916 gave impetus to further developments in school psychology. This event, along with the emergence of other tests of individual mental ability, provided the school psychologist with one of his major tools. Similarly the development of group tests, which first appeared during World War I—mainly as the result of the effort of Dr. Arthur S. Otis—spurred activity in psychological work.

Also significant in the development of school psychology was the mental hygiene movement and its journal, *Mental Hygiene*, which first appeared in 1917. According to Cutts:

---

[8] George E. Myers, *Principles and Techniques of Vocational Guidance* (New York: McGraw-Hill Book Company, Inc., 1941), p. 2.

The mental-hygiene movement and the emphasis on the importance of the early years of life and the "whole child" served to focus attention on the school as the first institution where work in mental hygiene might be done and on the work which the school psychologists were already doing. As a result some mental-hygiene and family-welfare societies collaborated with school psychologists to secure psychiatric and social work service for children.[9]

By 1920, school social work had become firmly recognized as a necessary part of the school program. The growth of the visiting teacher movement had been rapid among the eastern cities. Programs were being developed in several metropolitan areas in midwestern states—Kansas City, 1915; Indianapolis, 1916; and Chicago, 1919.

Considerable national interest in school social work was aroused in 1921, when the National Committee on Visiting Teachers, affiliated with the Public Education Association, was given a financial grant by the Commonwealth Fund of New York to conduct a nationwide demonstration and experiment in visiting teacher services. The project placed thirty visiting teachers in different city, town, and county schools to demonstrate the value of these services to education. The research which resulted provided some of the best descriptive and analytical material on school social work—specifically, four books: *The Visiting Teacher Movement, The Visiting Teacher in Rochester, The Problem Child in School,* and *The Visiting Teacher at Work.*[10]

The next decade in pupil personnel reflected a concern for new emphasis, and in all areas of pupil personnel there were efforts toward professional organization. In guidance a third significant period began about 1930: the clinical approach. Emphasis in guidance shifted to the individual and his capacities, abilities, interests, and character traits as they relate to occupational requirements.[11]

During this period, many new test publishing companies and educational research organizations were formed, such as the Psycho-

[9] Norma E. Cutts, ed., *School Psychologists at Mid-Century* (Washington, D.C.: American Psychological Association, Inc., 1955), p. 30.

[10] Katherine M. Cook, *The Place of Visiting Teacher Services in the School Program,* Federal Security Agency Bulletin 1945, No. 6 (Washington, D.C.: U.S. Government Printing Office, 1945), p. 8.

[11] Donald G. Paterson, "The Genesis of Modern Guidance," *Educational Record,* Vol. 19 (1938), pp. 36–46.

logical Corporation, The Educational Records Bureau, and the Institute of Educational Research at Columbia, and the University of Minnesota Testing Bureau. With World War II, personnel work in industry and the armed services increased.

School social workers throughout the nation were meeting together as a professional body as early as 1919, when the National Association of Visiting Teachers was formed to define and promote professional standards. After several changes in title, this group affiliated with the National Association of Social Workers in 1955, and became the school social work section of that body.

Although there has been growth in all aspects of the pupil personnel program, certification and training of specialists have not developed as rapidly as one might expect. National organizations such as the American Psychological Association, Division 16  (founded in 1947), the American Personnel and Guidance Association (founded in 1952), and others have taken on the responsibility of clarifying and defining the roles of specialists in this field.

## The Present Period of Coordinated Programs

As a result of the development of specialized services and the appearance in the school of specialists in pupil personnel work, schemes for coordinating these services have become increasingly necessary. In school systems throughout the nation, a variety of departments and divisions have been devised to perform this task. In addition to pupil personnel services, such titles as "special education," "guidance and child study services," "research services," and many others have appeared. There is currently a great deal of confusion resulting from the use of these different titles. Authorities, however, generally agree that the trend is toward using the title "pupil personnel." Similarly, within several states there is evidence of a trend toward using "pupil personnel" as the proper departmental designation for the coordination of these various services. California and New York, for example, have established divisions of pupil personnel within their state departments and have fostered similar departments in local school districts. In the last several years, the Office of Education of the United States Department of Health, Education, and Welfare has developed noticeably in this direction, having added job titles in pupil personnel to its roster.

# CHAPTER IV

# Responsibilities of the
# School Staff in Pupil Personnel

Pupil personnel requires the attention of all members of the school staff. Several aspects of the work are general responsibilities of school administrators and classroom teachers and are inseparable from their administrative and classroom duties. It is difficult to separate, for example, a teacher's responsibilities for guidance and for keeping pupil records from his daily classroom teaching activities. Also, every teacher is to some degree conducting a child-study program for he is continuously studying the learner.

## The Role of School Administrators

The school administrator is responsible for coordinating this phase of the school program with other phases. His also is the vital responsibility of resolving problems of staff and budget and relationships with the board of education. One might even say that the administrator's is the most important role in determining whether or not effective pupil personnel services will exist.

Pupil personnel responsibilities of the different levels of school administration vary markedly. The superintendent, for example, has a very different role from that of the school principal.

*Superintendents.* The superintendent is, in large measure, the person responsible for the quality of pupil personnel services. If he is sympathetic and vigorous in his support, the program will prosper and services will be adequate. The most effective programs are found where the superintendent understands the developmental aims and the spirit of the modern pupil personnel concept. In addition to giving general support, there are many specific ways in which the superintendent manifests the value he places on these services.

Employing competent staff to carry out the many pupil personnel functions is a first specific responsibility of the superintendent. The astute superintendent recognizes that selecting a director of pupil personnel is one of his most important decisions. The person selected must be an administrator himself, yet one who is thoroughly familiar with and experienced in the work of pupil personnel. He must be able to see these services both as specialities and as integral aspects of the overall school program.

A second responsibility of the superintendent is to keep the administrative lines clear so the director of pupil personnel and his staff will at all times understand their relationship to other parts of the school program and other workers. He must define the responsibilities of the director so that his activities can be coordinated with those of other administrators on the central office staff. The superintendent is obligated to see that the entire pupil personnel program is clearly outlined and clearly understood by the school staff. He must guard against making pupil personnel a "special services" department. In some school systems, the pupil personnel department becomes the headquarters for any school activity which does not seem to fit logically some other department. The superintendent must make clear to the staff exactly what special jobs are to be done by pupil personnel.

The superintendent has responsibility for providing office space for pupil personnel and seeing that adequate budget is provided. He relies heavily upon the director to keep him informed of the department's budgetary needs and for recommendations on a reasonable expenditure for programs and new developments.

To keep the program up to date and functioning smoothly, the superintendent must constantly evaluate its operation. Together with the director, he must realign the several services and the specialists to meet the changing needs of the school system. To conduct this essential role effectively, he regularly calls upon the director and the various staff members of pupil personnel to inform him orally and in writing on the progress of the department.

Acting as the chief officer of the board of education, the superintendent is responsible for recommending an adequate set of rules and regulations to govern the policies and the activities of the school. Included in these policies will be several which directly involve pupil personnel, such as statements concerning the implementation of a program of school attendance. School attendance operates within a framework of state statutes which must be enforced by the boards of education in local school districts. The board, under advisement from the superintendent, is responsible for establishing the ways in which the attendance function will be administered. The superintendent is responsible for carrying out the policies once they have been established. To do this job effectively requires implementing not simply the letter of the law, but also the spirit and intent of the law. In years past a superintendent might have regarded school attendance laws statistically and impersonally, putting the major emphasis on noncompliance as a breaking of the law and a threat to the school budget. Today, however, pupil attendance policies are written and implemented through an enlightened pupil personnel approach whose primary purpose is to provide a school program geared to the needs of the pupils and which will insure against any child being denied schooling.

The modern superintendent also administers with great care the exemptions from school attendance. He does not, for example, permit an abuse of the suspension or expulsion laws which, without judicious concern, can be used to remove youngsters from school. Nor does he permit the use of dismissal laws, which are usually based upon a child's inability to profit from the school program for reasons of low mental ability, to stand between the child and the school's obligation to adjust a program to his needs. Similarly, he is careful that the work permit program is carefully administered to advantage of the child and the community rather than as a vehicle to rid the school of some of its problems.

Assigning children to instructional programs from which they will derive optimum benefit is the responsibility of the superintendent. For 85 per cent of the youngsters in the typical school system, this is a rather routine and mechanical operation for it can be based upon age and grades completed. Fifteen per cent of the student population, however, is made up of pupils who are in need of special educational programing and assignment. For these youngsters more careful consideration and planning must occur. These are the children who are physically or mentally handicapped or who demonstrate behavioral difficulties. In carrying out his responsibility for assigning children into the proper school program, the superintendent relies upon pupil personnel. They advise him about special assignments which are appropriate for individual children and about

which need to be developed. In a program for the
ally retarded, for example, careful identification and
ust precede assignment.

only a few of the more important ways in which the
ent is responsible for pupil personnel. They show him
important functionary in carrying out an effective pupil
program with the aid of the information and services of
his sta...

*Principals.* The principal of the elementary or secondary school is responsible for all of the activities that go on in his building. Chief among his responsibilities is the maintenance of a climate which is conducive to effective pupil personnel work. The principal must possess a favorable attitude which he must endeavor to reflect in his relations with teachers so that they too will carry out their pupil personnel responsibilities more effectively.

The principal must coordinate the programs of all pupil personnel specialists in his building and encourage the use of these specialists by the teachers. He must help the various specialists to interpret themselves and their programs to his teaching staff. He must provide time so the specialists can work with the teachers on the problems of individuals who have been referred to them for study. He must also use the pupil personnel specialists for developing greater staff effectiveness by arranging for in-service workshops and seminars where teachers can learn more about matters of child growth and development, measurement, and the handling of behavior problems.

The principal has many other responsibilities in this area. Some of these are interpreting pupil progress to parents, conducting age-grade studies within the building, making careful studies where there is a question of a child being retained or promoted, coordinating a program of achievement and ability testing, and maintaining pupil discipline.[1]

Other pupil personnel responsibilities include maintaining pupil

---

[1] Although discipline is not a responsibility of pupil personnel, behavior for which special controls must be exercised is often merely the symptom of a troubled child. It is not unusual for an elementary school child to show an exaggerated need for attention when the arrival of a new baby in the home threatens his position. He may even set about trying to be sent home, where he can protect his position.

records and conducting a program to keep nonattendance to a minimum. At times it is the teacher who carries out the details, but the principal is finally responsible for everything that goes on in his building. His effectiveness in discharging these particular responsibilities depends upon his having the pupil personnel point of view and also upon his making wise use of the specialists from the pupil personnel department.

## The Role of Teachers

The teacher is a major functionary in the total pupil personnel program. Strang lists several of the distinguishing characteristics by which one can tell when the teacher has accepted pupil personnel and is making it function effectively in his relations with pupils. These characteristics are:

1. If he can maintain a relationship of trust and confidence even though he has to disapprove of student's conduct.

2. If he can help a student to achieve a clearer idea of his more acceptable self, a sense of direction, and hope for the future.

3. If he can persuade adults and others in the student's immediate environment to accept the best of him.

4. If he can discover the student's most pressing needs and make provisions for them by using resources in the school and the community.

5. If he can build on the positive elements in the situation and never deprive the student of his few legitimate satisfactions.

6. If he can learn enough about the new student to help him "get off to a new start," rather than neglect him until serious problems demand attention.

7. If he can gradually get the personnel point of view accepted and practiced by other members of the faculty and by students.[2]

The exact role of the teacher in pupil personnel work is not a simple clear-cut matter. The number and the nature of his responsibilities vary according to many conditions, such as the specialists who are available. Generally, where there is a well-organized and well-staffed department of pupil personnel, the teacher's responsibilities are lessened. However, this is not always the case, for some

---

[2] Ruth Strang, *The Role of the Teacher in Guidance and Personnel Work,* rev. ed. (New York: Bureau of Publications, Teachers College, Columbia University, 1946), p. 25.

school systems regard the teacher as being directly responsible for all of the pupil personnel duties in connection with his class. This has been and continues to be a controversial issue.

The disagreement is essentially whether or not the specialities of pupil personnel, such as guidance and child study, are more adequately performed by the classroom teacher in his daily contacts with children or whether they should be carried out by specialists.

Those who support the latter point of view contend that the competencies required are so technical that it is unreasonable to expect the teacher to learn them without a great deal of additional training. Further, they contend that the job of instruction is too important and demanding to permit a teacher to perform both functions effectively.

Common practice is for the teacher to carry out many of the pupil personnel jobs but with a certain number of counselors, psychologists, and social workers available to help in case of more extreme need.

This controversy, for the present at least, does not apply to many of the traditional pupil personnel tasks which have always made up a substantial part of the teacher's daily activities and for which he invariably has responsibility. These are ones where pupil personnel workers enter the picture only to provide special assistance or to coordinate the efforts of teachers in one school with those in other schools.

Teachers, for example, usually are the connecting link between the pupil in school and the home. Even with the appearance of the school social worker, the teacher's need to keep in touch with the home is not negated. Reporting pupil progress, keeping records of attendance, and handling behavior and conduct problems are virtually inseparable parts of the teacher's classroom work. In some situations the teacher's responsibility includes keeping the cumulative records and making appropriate entries in them from time to time.

More in question are the personnel responsibilities of recent origin, but even here certain aspects are extremely difficult to separate from the teacher's instructional duties. Whether or not specialists might be available, teachers invariably are called upon to do some individual child study, group testing, and counseling with children who have personal or social problems.

Stoops and others list twenty rather specific responsibilities of the teacher in personnel work which have occurred as a result of the expanding American education program. Some of these are:

1. Observe and identify symptoms of physical illness and sensory defect.
2. Recognize and consult with attendance and welfare counselors on problems pertaining to conditions in the home.
3. Identify pupils needing special study and request assistance with them.
4. Analyze the physical, emotional, and educational needs of pupils in the classroom.
5. Help parents to increase their understanding of the child's needs.
6. Perform group guidance services in the areas of study skills, social-adjustment skills, and certain types of occupational information and self-appraisal activities, relating the classroom work to specifications of appropriate occupations.
7. Participate in child-study groups and other workshops in which the teacher gains insights and understandings of his own behavior needs and those of the pupil.
8. Maintain a record on each pupil with appropriate entries of test data, course marks, observations, handicaps, and anecdotal accounts of pertinent information for recording on the cumulative record.
9. Evaluate, in co-operation with the counselor, each pupil's educational and vocational plan.
10. Help pupils discover their abilities and limitations.
11. Encourage pupils to utilize counseling services.[3]

Entire texts have been written on the role of the teacher in pupil personnel work, notably by Strang,[4] and more recently one by Johnson, Peters, and Evraiff.[5] A particularly clear statement about the responsibility of the teacher is offered in Yeager [6] who points to the positive aspects of the teacher in pupil personnel. A teacher must be poised and serene and respect the individuality of each child. He must help children to develop positive goals, ways to evaluate themselves, and behavior controls.

[3] Emery Stoops, ed., *Guidance Services: Organization and Administration* (New York: McGraw-Hill Book Company, Inc., 1959), pp. 133–34.

[4] Ruth Strang, *op. cit.*

[5] Edgar G. Johnson, Mildred Peters, and William Evraiff, *The Role of the Teacher in Guidance* (Englewood Cliffs, N.J.: Prentice-Hall, Inc., 1959).

[6] William A. Yeager, *Administration and the Pupil* (New York: Harper & Row, Publishers, 1949), p. 188.

# CHAPTER V

# Organization and Coordination
# of Pupil Personnel Services

## Progress in the Development of Departments

Increased attention to pupil needs and to provisions to insure optimum pupil development have brought about vast increases in the number and quality of pupil personnel services. Educators and laymen have recognized the need for specially trained workers to provide these services and an administrative structure to facilitate their effective use by teachers and pupils. The result in many school districts and state departments of education has been the creation of a department of pupil personnel. The procurement of personnel, the assignment of duties and responsibilities, the development of channels of communication and evaluation, and the coordination of pupil personnel with instruction and administration are developments which are continuously resulting from the rapid growth and expansion of these services.

Actually, provisions to coordinate programs are even more recent than the development of the individual services in most school districts. Much of the growth has occurred since 1930. A comparison of the earliest departments with those of the last thirty years reveals broad changes in departmental or organizational names and in the number and kinds of services being coordinated. Earlier administrative units were primarily concerned with attendance functions and bore such titles as Bureau of Compulsory Attendance, Department of Compulsory Attendance, or Attendance Department. As early as 1929, however, emphasis toward a broader concept was appearing. In that year one of the leading texts in the field was published which recommended the development of departments of pupil personnel.[1] Since then the breadth, quality, and number of pupil personnel

---

[1] Arch O. Heck, *Administration of Pupil Personnel* (New York: Ginn and Company, 1929), pp. 101–102.

departments have shown a definite increase. Where earlier departments were often dominated by attendance activities, a shift toward a broader base of responsibilities has occurred. Even the attendance aspect has shifted away from "legal enforcement of school attendance to removal or amelioration of pupil adjustment." [2]

By 1960, Voorhees [3] claims, approximately 70 per cent of the school districts in Indiana, Michigan, and Ohio with populations between 25,000 and 100,000 developed departments of pupil personnel or such departments as Pupil Personnel and Special Services, Pupil Personnel and Special Education, or Pupil Personnel and Research. Furthermore, he learned, the majority of the school districts which did not have departments indicated plans to form them.

Along with developments in local school districts, there has also been "a nation-wide trend toward the establishment of Departments of Pupil Personnel at the state level." [4] This observation resulted from a study conducted at Michigan State University in 1957 in which every state and territorial possession of the United States was surveyed to determine whether or not such a department existed. The study also revealed that there "was no evidence of abandonment of such a department once it had been provided; rather every indication was of past and future expansion of services." [5]

A primary responsibility of state departments of education has been to develop administrative procedures for implementing educational programs in local school districts. Often this includes maintaining a well-staffed and coordinated division of pupil personnel which has as one of its tasks the provision of services for school districts which cannot afford an adequate staff of their own. With the increased development of local programs, state departments of education are also playing a significant role in helping local districts with their concerns about expansion of services. State personnel meet with local officials to evaluate pupil personnel programs and to devise more effective arrangements for coordina-

---

[2] Arch O. Heck, "Pupil Personnel," *Encyclopedia of Educational Research*, rev. ed. (New York: The Macmillan Company, 1950), p. 912.

[3] Leonard B. Voorhees, "A Descriptive Study of the Organization, Administration, and Operation of Pupil Personnel Services in Selected School Districts" (Doctoral dissertation presented at Michigan State University, 1960), pp. 81–82.

[4] Voorhees, "A Descriptive Study of Pupil Personnel Services," p. 52.

[5] *Ibid.*

tion and administration. Consultation is provided by highly trained state specialists to help the local school system decide upon questions of staff expansion and the reallocation of existing staff to provide a better use of the time and energy of the specialists.

As early as 1949, Yeager [6] discussed many demands that were being made on state departments of education for additional services, pointing out how their scope has been considerably enlarged. More and more state specialists are spending time in the local school districts consulting on guidance, school health, social work, and other problems.

*Organizational patterns in pupil personnel.* No single "best" system of organization exists which solves all of the school's need for administrative structure and leadership. Each school district, however, should develop some kind of organizational framework to be sure that the pupil personnel services function smoothly, that specialists are properly assigned, and that the services are coordinated with one another and with other aspects of the school program.

The considerations which determine the framework for administering and organizing these services differ from district to district. Authorities, however, generally agree that the size of the school district, availability of specialists, financial circumstances, interests and special competencies of existing staff, and local traditions and administrative philosophy are of greatest importance.

Large school districts, for example, often have complicated organizational structure because of the many services provided and the number of specialists required to carry them out. In districts such as Chicago, Cleveland, New York City, and Baltimore the programs are so large and complicated that several administrators are employed. A deputy superintendent or assistant superintendent will usually be made responsible for the administration of the broad area of pupil personnel and will report directly to the superintendent. Reporting to him will be directors of departments or bureaus of guidance, psychological services, or attendance services. In small districts, usually found in rural areas, the scope of services provided is often small and the number of specialists very limited. The national trend, however, appears to be toward consolidation of small school districts. Some are being replaced by intermediate adminis-

---

6 William A. Yeager, *Administration and the Pupil* (New York: Harper & Row, Publishers, 1949), pp. 463–64.

trative and service units such as New York State's Boards of Cooperative Educational Services.

At present the most clear-cut departmental arrangements seem to exist in school districts with student populations ranging from 10,000 to 15,000. In districts of this size, departments of pupil personnel services are fairly common. These departments at times bear titles such as Guidance and Child Study, Special Services, or even Special Education, but the term Pupil Personnel seems to be appearing with increasing frequency. When the U.S. Office of Education undertook a study of the organization and administration of pupil personnel services, it selected eight school districts with populations ranging between 7,000 and 15,000 students. The study indicated fairly distinct administrative arrangements. Specialists in the five major pupil personnel areas—attendance, guidance, health, psychological, and social work—were ". . . administratively responsible to a director of the program; an assistant superintendent for instruction; or the superintendent of school." [7]

Shibler [8] discusses three levels of organizational structure within present programs. The least organized occurs where the services operate exclusive of one another; at the other extreme is the "multiple plan" with a high degree of coordination. The midground is described as the "semimultiple plan."

Authorities generally oppose arrangements where the services operate without coordination. Similarly, the multiple plan, although desirable in many ways, is considered to be unrealistic by many school administrators because of the expense involved and the difficulty in obtaining an ample number of well-trained specialists. In such a plan pupil diagnostic and treatment functions receive very careful attention and the number of specialists in psychology, social work, medical services, and counseling is large. Although teachers and administrators agree generally that well-staffed and carefully implemented programs are desirable, few school systems to date have been able to support such patterns.

---

[7] Gene C. Fusco, *Organization and Administration of Pupil Personnel Service Programs in Selected School Systems* (Washington, D.C.: U.S. Department of Health, Education, and Welfare, 1961).

[8] Herman L. Shibler, "Organization of Personnel Services," in *Personnel Services in Education,* Fifty-Eighth Yearbook of the National Society for the Study of Education, Part II, ed. Nelson B. Henry (Chicago: The University of Chicago Press, 1959), p. 158.

There seems to be little doubt but that a trend exists toward the development of departments or similar administrative units to administer programs of pupil personnel. This does not mean, however, that the title "pupil personnel" or, in fact, the need for a coordinated program of services is universally accepted. Some objections to the departmental concept have been financial; others are even deeper and relate to questions of philosophy and point of view. Not uncommon, for example, is the claim that it is unnecessary to have specialists in the school to do a job that really belongs to teachers and principal. Another opinion agrees on the value of specialists but argues that rather than have these pupil personnel workers coordinated in a single department, a more effective arrangement is for them to be assigned directly to individual school buildings where they will be working. This point of view reflects the belief of teachers and principals that such specialists can be most effectively used if they are readily available as needs arise.

Generally, administrators and specialists who have had experience in the field of pupil personnel work oppose the building-centered concept. They claim, for one thing, that it is financially unrealistic to provide specialists in most of the pupil personnel areas for individual schools. Also the lack of an adequate supply of trained specialists precludes such an organizational approach, although it is recognized that the assignment of specialists to individual schools on a weekly or bi-weekly basis has worked successfully in some school districts. Other objections to the building-centered approach relate to the possible misuse of the time and energy of the specialists, as ". . . the worker reports directly to a school principal who sees the specialist as one more available 'hand' to assign to yard duty, study halls, policing athletic events, or substitute teaching." [9]

## The Specialists in Pupil Personnel Administration

Along with the development of departments of pupil personnel there has been an inevitable emergence of a new administrator: the director of pupil personnel. This officer is called by various titles depending upon the nature of his responsibilities and on the title

---

[9] Raymond N. Hatch and Buford Stefflre, *Administration of Guidance Services: Organization, Supervision, Evaluation* (Englewood Cliffs, N.J.: Prentice-Hall, Inc., 1958), p. 107.

of the department. Generally individuals who are in such positions of responsibility have had experience and training both in school administration and in one of several of the areas of pupil personnel specialization.

The exact responsibilities of the director vary, but essentially his duties are administrative and include selection of staff, the provision of time and facilities, clarification of the roles of the specialists, and interpretation and overall evaluation of programs. "The director of the division," Shibler points out, "must deal with interpretation of established policy and is the final authority for the determination of relative jurisdiction of the services offered by the division." [10] Besides this decision-making responsibility, however, he must also work with others in a nonauthoritarian, service, or facilitating capacity. Pupil personnel services are essentially facilitative, their job being to see that pupils receive optimum benefit from the educational program by providing services to teachers and principals and often directly to the pupils themselves. Administrative leadership through a nonauthoritarian, helping approach is by no means unique to pupil personnel administration, but it is critically important since these services often involve consultation rather than exercise of authority.

Specific training programs and certification standards for administrators of pupil personnel are very rare. In a recent study, 32 major universities were asked what specific training programs they had for administrators of pupil personnel. None had a specific program to prepare pupil personnel administrators. Several indicated that although they at present had no doctoral programs in pupil personnel administration, they were making some plans in this direction. The majority of the 32 universities had well-organized counselor training programs and several of them trained school psychologists. Within these programs special administrative courses and practicum were provided for those who aspired to administration, but these generally were only appropriate for a specific area of pupil personnel. [11]

It appears that there is a trend toward the establishment of specific training patterns and certification for administrative specialists in pupil personnel. Only four states—Kentucky, Maryland, Massa-

---

[10] Shibler, "Organization of Personnel Services," p. 154.
[11] Unpublished study by the author, 1961.

chusetts, and New York—have had specific statutory provisions for administrators of pupil personnel.[12] A more recent development are the specific certificates which only a few states have to date. Ohio, for example, certificates supervisors in school psychology, counseling, and also in the broader overall field of pupil personnel. Beginning in 1964, it will institute an administrative assistant's certificate in pupil personnel.[13] Other states as well are making progress in this direction.

---

[12] Winston L. Roesch, *Statutory Basis for Administrative and Specialized Service Staffing in Local School Districts* (Washington, D.C.: U.S. Department of Health, Education, and Welfare, 1959), p. 31.

[13] Ohio, State Department of Education, *Laws and Regulations Governing the Certification of Teachers, Administrators, Supervisors, and School Employees in Pupil Personnel Service* (Columbus, Ohio: The F. J. Heer Printing Company, 1962), p. 49.

# CHAPTER VI

# Counseling and Guidance Services

Guidance is the most rapidly developing area of all pupil personnel services. Despite its newness (it first appeared in the early 1900's), there are more workers in this area than in any other area of personnel work. Certainly, more public notice and attention in professional literature is being given to guidance than to any of the other pupil personnel services. Guidance workers are very much in demand at the present time, and the need for them far exceeds the supply of trained workers. Guidance is the broader area of pupil personnel service which includes counseling. Consequently, a school guidance worker might do some counseling as well as other jobs of guidance. On the other hand, "school counselor" is the title which more frequently designates a highly trained specialist who spends at least half his time counseling with pupils.

## The Program of Guidance Services

Guidance services are provided in the schools to help the pupil to know and understand himself and to use this understanding in making plans and decisions for the future. They also aid his attaining better mental health and a fuller use of his capacities through insight and a clear understanding of his interaction with the people and the circumstances in which he finds himself. They are provided as part of the school's attempt to insure optimum pupil development. Authorities generally agree on what services should make up the guidance program. Although new ideas are constantly occurring along with shifts in emphasis on one activity or another, the basic service remains fairly stable. The modern guidance program includes counseling of individuals, group guidance, orientation, educational and vocational guidance, individual inventories, and placement and follow-up.

One author discusses guidance from the standpoint of its three major functions: adjustive, distributive, and adaptive. The adjustive

39

function concerns diagnosis and treatment. Working in a one-to-one relationship, the counselor attempts to help the student with difficulties that are adversely affecting his adjustment in school. The distributive function entails collecting and distributing occupational and educational information and helping students reach vocational and educational decisions. In his adaptive function, the guidance counselor serves the school as a whole, his purpose being to point out ways in which the school needs to change in order to adapt more adequately to the pupil.[1]

*Counseling.* As guidance currently operates, the counseling function is viewed as its major service. Much modern guidance literature is devoted to defining and clarifying the counseling role in education.[2] It is generally viewed as a process involving direct contact between a pupil and a counselor aimed at assisting the pupil to adjust more effectively to himself and his environment.

For example, a senior student is aware that he faces military duty and that there is an alternative of entering now or after college. More information and help are needed before he can make his decision. This student might also have some personal fears about military service or anxiety about an interruption of his education. The school counselor can help him to obtain the information needed and to decide on a course of action. Also, the counselor will help him explore his anxieties and establish more positive feelings about the nature and value of military service.

Formerly, counseling was viewed primarily as a technique used in helping youngsters make vocational and educational choices. Now, with an emphasis on social and emotional factors in learning, on the total personality, and on the influence of culture in determining pupil development, counseling is seen as a way of helping with the broad range of questions and concerns that pupils face as part of growing up. No longer is it viewed merely as a technique and limited to vocational and educational matters; counseling is regarded as the central service in the guidance program. Some even claim that ". . . the counselor is the major factor in the effectiveness

---

[1] Henry B. McDaniel, *Guidance in the Modern School* (New York: Holt, Rinehart & Winston, Inc., 1956), pp. 12–13.

[2] Lyle D. Schmidt, "Concepts of the Role of Secondary School Counselors," *Personnel and Guidance Journal*, XL, No. 7 (1962), 600–605; and Harold B. Pepinsky and Pauline N. Pepinsky, *Counseling: Theory and Practice* (New York: The Ronald Press Co., 1954).

of any pupil personnel program and the program is best seen in relation to him." [3]

This new emphasis has come about in large measure as a result of explorations in the aims of American education, particularly the objective of self-realization. Although educators are just beginning to explore the real meaning of self-realization, it is apparent that the concept involves more than simply realization in reading, writing, and the other academic skills. In addition, it relates to the learner's developing fully his potential for rich living and citizenship through better self-understanding. Much more than intellectual skill is required for adjustment in today's fast moving and highly complicated world.

Psychology and sociology for years have been contributing to our understanding of emotional and social factors in the adjustment of individuals and groups. Their influence is being reflected in the new prominence given to counseling services in American elementary and secondary schools. More and more counselor trainees are being required to obtain thorough grounding in personality theory, social theory, and course work in the dynamics of human behavior before beginning training in the techniques and practices of counseling. It is not at all uncommon today to find graduate programs of counselor education in departments of educational psychology or counseling psychology. Trainers and students alike are requesting that more attention be given to the psychological and sociological foundations of counselor training programs. A recent study conducted by Polmantier and Schmidt [4] analyzing the number and kind of courses in the counselor training program of 54 state universities indicates that the most frequently offered course—other than the basic course in guidance—is in methods and techniques of counseling. The need for more course and practicum experience in counseling was cited as the major recommendation in a study by Harmon and Arnold [5] in which counselors were asked to evaluate their formal preparation.

[3] C. Gilbert Wrenn, *The Counselor in a Changing World* (Washington, D.C.: American Personnel and Guidance Association, 1962), p. 111.

[4] Paul C. Polmantier and Lyle D. Schmidt, "Areas of Preparation for School Guidance Workers," *The Personnel and Guidance Journal*, Vol. XXXIX, No. 1 (September, 1960), 45–46.

[5] Donald Harmon and Dwight L. Arnold, "High School Counselors Evaluate Their Formal Preparation," *The Personnel and Guidance Journal*, Vol. XXXIX, No. 4 (December, 1960), 303–306.

A third influence responsible for the new emphasis in counseling obtains from the many professional workers who are concerned with the confusion which now surrounds the term "guidance." Their concern is for a clarification of terms to increase the professionalization of school counseling. A statement by Pierson and Grant clearly expresses this point of view:

> Personnel and guidance workers should build their profession around the concept "counselor" rather than around the concept "guidance worker." The objectives of the guidance movement in education have remained so general and so comprehensive during the past fifty years that guidance is still mainly a point of view, a pervasive influence, a belief in the importance of individualized education. Only occasionally does the word guidance refer to a truly significant program of services. The writers of this article are convinced that the term guidance should be set free for the use of anyone in education who believes that the student must be *known and dealt with as a person* and that personnel and guidance specialists should put forth every effort to make the school counselor a genuine professional worker.[6]

*Group guidance.* Group guidance has essentially the same objectives as the individual counseling program. Group guidance programs often include formal classes, informal group discussions, student government and activity groups, small group counseling, and special guest lecture series.

In a class setting pupils are helped to develop self-direction and independence in making educational and vocational decisions. They are also helped to mature in personal-social aspects of life. Opportunities are provided in group guidance sessions for pupils to discuss and explore common problems of growing up. Through the leadership of a guidance-orientated teacher or counselor, pupils develop insight into personality dynamics and are aided in a redirection of their own energy toward a resolution, or at least lessening, of some of their concerns and problems. One eleventh grade class in group guidance, for example, conducted a "problem census" in which all of the youngsters spoke about the things that concerned them most. The counselor made a list of these problems and then —with the group—reclassified the list, arriving at several concerns

---

[6] George A. Pierson and Claude W. Grant, "The Road Ahead for the School Counselor," *The Personnel and Guidance Journal,* Vol. XXXVIII, No. 3 (November, 1959), 207.

which the majority of the pupils felt it would be helpful to explore. Over 50 per cent of the pupils asked questions such as: how much money should eleventh graders be expected to spend in a week, should they be expected to work for their money, what was the average amount of money youngsters their age had to spend, and how important was the money in gaining attention, favor, and respect? The group felt that one approach to exploring these questions might be to ask each member of the class to answer a questionnaire. The questionnaire was devised and administered; then the answers were organized in table form showing the average and range of pupil responses to each of the questions. The pupils were helped to see whether their situation was close to the average, or above or below average. A value of such group guidance discussions frequently cited by pupils is the opportunity to find out what problems other children are facing. Pupils confide that it is helpful to know that their classmates share the same kinds of problems and concerns.

One of the chief values of group guidance activities is their economy. Experts often comment on the effectiveness of group methods for collecting and distributing information helpful to pupils. Most of the school's standardized testing program, for example, can be administered on a group basis. Pupils in a group guidance class can take school ability, achievement, aptitude, and interest tests, score them and then record their own results. Under the leadership of a counselor, even some group interpretation of the test results is possible. Other valuable outcomes of group guidance activities are the identification of pupils who need special help and the preparation of pupils for individual counseling. One authority notes that an important function of group procedures in guidance is the ". . . preparation of pupils for effective participation in the counseling process." [7]

*Orientation.* Guidance orientation activities are designed to help students become familiar with the overall school situation such as the teaching and administrative staff, the physical plant, the curriculum, the policies and procedures for governing student conduct,

---

[7] Margaret E. Bennett, "Functions and Procedures in Personnel Services," in *Personnel Services in Education,* Fifty-Eighth Yearbook of the National Society for the Study of Education, Part II, ed. Nelson B. Henry (Chicago: The University of Chicago Press, 1959), p. 130.

and the student activity program. A purpose in orientation is to help pupils make effective adjustments during certain critical transition periods in their school lives. Guidance records reveal that these points occur as pupils move from home into their first school experience, from primary grades to the upper elementary grades, from elementary to junior high school, from junior high school to senior high school, and finally from senior to post high school life. A well-planned program of orientation can help them to adjust and make better use of the experiences which lie ahead.

The orientation program usually includes discussions with the counselor or home room teacher, discussion and tours with upper class pupils, and assemblies. At times orientation topics are incorporated into group guidance classes where pupils are provided with information about school and also are given an opportunity to discuss the reasons underlying the school's rules and requirements. Like group guidance, orientation activities often lead to a pupil's arranging for individual counseling. Through orientation activities he has an opportunity to meet with the counselor and learn about ways in which the counseling program can help him to get the most out of his school experience. Many of the activities of the guidance program—such as individual counseling, group guidance, and orientation activities—blend imperceptibly one into the other, leading to a richer and more meaningful school experience for the student.

*Educational and vocational guidance.* Guidance came into the school primarily to perform educational and vocational functions. In them the counselor seeks to help the student make wise choices and decisions concerning the selection of a vocation and the selection of educational programs. These continue to be very important functions in the guidance program and aspects which involve a major share of the counselor's time. In the secondary schools much of guidance and personnel work relates directly or indirectly to these functions; the collection and distribution of occupational information, the testing program, and the placement and follow-up activities are all designed to help pupils make and follow vocational and educational plans.

Deciding upon whether or not to go to college, selecting a college, and finding a scholarship or some other sort of financial assistance are all very common concerns among today's secondary school pupils. In our society almost any youth who graduates from high school can go to college, but often he needs educational guidance in order to clarify and accomplish his aims. He needs a concerned and informed person with whom to discuss his plans and to explore catalogues, application forms, scholarship forms, and entrance examinations and requirements. In school districts where the majority of the student population goes on to college, as much as 80 per cent and more of the counselor's time is involved in education guidance.

The nation in general needs a well-informed citizenry. Also, with technical advances occurring at a rapid pace, the nation's manpower needs require a higher degree of technical competence among persons entering the labor market. Much of the responsibility for providing this rests with the educational institution and vocational and educational guidance services. Recently a great deal of concern has been expressed about the large number of youngsters capable of completing high school and entering college who are stopping at high school graduation or in some instances even dropping out before they graduate. This represents a great loss of potentially skilled manpower and a challenge to guidance workers and other educators.

*Individual inventory.* Individual inventory involves the efforts of the entire school staff and the keeping and analyzing of pupil records, particularly the cumulative records. Its purpose is to collect and make available a variety of information about each pupil which will enable the school staff to plan an optimum educational program for him. Through pupil observation, interview, testing, sociometric analysis, and other techniques, information is collected and made available to teachers, counselors, and others. Information recorded will vary from one school to another but will typically include school marks achieved throughout the school experience, comments concerning general factors of adjustment, facts describing curricular and extracurricular activities, medical history, and social adjustment data. Concerning this function, Hutson states, "The guidance program must include activities calculated to bring about a complete knowledge of the individual pupil by all who are responsible for his guidance." [8]

Some counselors are exploring the feasibility and value of having pupils use cumulative record information. One counselor, for ex-

---

[8] Percival W. Hutson, *The Guidance Function in Education* (New York: Appleton-Century-Crofts, Inc., 1958), p. 327.

ample, has developed a separate cumulative record to which pupils have supervised access. Many kinds of information about the pupil are recorded, such as some standardized test results, past grades, records of interests and hobbies, and even teacher evaluation forms. This experiment, the counselor believes, encourages pupils to collect and use information about themselves. After a time, many pupils can be taught to use such records independent of counselor supervision.

*Placement and follow-up.* Through placement and follow-up, the school assists pupils to follow through on their choices and decisions in vocational and educational planning. As a result pupils are often aided in achieving admittance to colleges of their choice, to a business or trade school or in entering the world of work.

Follow-up studies of guidance also provide evaluative information on the basis of which the effectiveness of the total school program can be appraised. This is accomplished through the use of questionnaires, interviews, and other data-collecting devices which record the opinions of employers, college officials, and pupils who have graduated or quit school before graduation. Information thus gained helps school officials to determine whether pupils are being well prepared for requirements they will face in college or on the job. Such information often leads to curriculum revisions or to the development of new instruction methods and programs.

## Growth in Guidance Services

No aspect of the pupil personnel program is growing more rapidly than guidance. Several factors account for this—among them the reports written by James Conant [9] on the American high school and junior high school emphasizing the need for counselors. Unquestionably, the greatest boost to guidance that has ever occurred resulted from the National Defense Education Act of 1958, which pointed it out as a necessary and vital part of American education. Even more tangible has been the appropriation of millions of dollars by the federal government through the National Defense Education Act to support several aspects of guidance and of counselor

---

[9] James B. Conant, *The American High School Today* (New York: McGraw-Hill Book Company, Inc., 1959), pp. 44–45; and James B. Conant, *A Memorandum to School Boards: Recommendations for Education in the Junior High School Years* (Princeton, N.J.: Educational Testing Service, 1960), p. 27.

training. One section of this Act provides funds to improve guidance, counseling, and testing services in American secondary schools. It authorizes the government to contract with institutions of higher education to conduct institutes for training teachers to become guidance counselors and also for upgrading persons who presently are employed as counselors.

A newsletter of the American Personnel and Guidance Association summarizes some of the effects upon guidance of the National Defense Education Act:

> Fifty states, the District of Columbia and the three territories are participating in the guidance, counseling, and testing program under this phase of the 1958 bill . . . . Specifically, progress is noted in reducing student-counselor ratios. In 1953, for example, the ratio of counselors to students was estimated at 1 to 750. By June 1960, it was estimated that this ratio had decreased to 1 to 600. Much of this reduction is attributed to the fact that approximately 90 per cent of Title V-A funds are being used to pay salaries of counselors.[10]

The same article further discusses the advances that have been made in group testing programs resulting from the Act and points out that substantial growth also has taken place in the number of new state guidance supervisors employed. With respect to state guidance personnel, it comments: "There were 78 directors or supervisors of guidance employed by state educational agencies before 1958. Records in the United States Office of Education presently indicate that there are approximately 183 state personnel carrying out full-time guidance responsibilities."[11]

Testimony to this tremendous growth can also be seen in local school districts and in state-wide summaries. In Ohio, for example, between the 1958–59 and 1959–60 school years, there was an increase of 10 per cent in the number of school districts to develop counseling programs. During the same year, the number of counseling units jumped from 323 to 511 throughout the state, and the counselor-pupil ratio was reduced from 1:552 to 1:426.[12] These gains are typical of the nationwide pattern.

*Guidance in elementary schools.* Another noteworthy develop-

---

[10] Arthur A. Hitchcock, ed., *The Guidepost,* Vol. III, No. 2 (Washington, D.C.: American Personnel and Guidance Association, Inc., December, 1960), p. 1.

[11] Hitchcock, *The Guidepost,* p. 1.

[12] Dean L. Hummel, ed., *Ohio Guidance News and Views,* Vol. X, No. 3 (Columbus, Ohio: State Department of Education, Division of Guidance and Testing, 1960), p. 1.

ment is the movement of guidance into elementary schools. Until recently guidance programs had been limited to secondary schools, but they are now beginning to appear in elementary schools with a new specialist, the elementary school counselor.

There is agreement regarding the need for guidance at this level, but two very different points of view exist on what guidance functions would be proper and on who should perform them. On one hand are those who view guidance as an aspect of the pupil personnel program in which specialists are identified and specific guidance services are indicated. The position held by advocates of this approach is clearly stated in Cottingham: "The services normally comprise the individual inventory, counseling, information services, placement and follow-up, and are sometimes expanded to include group procedures and research." [13] It is recognized that the organization as well as emphasis of these services will be different from those typically found in high school, since elementary school needs differ from those of the secondary school.

Also supporting the "services and specialists" approach is the California State Department of Education which describes elementary school guidance as a team effort. In a bulletin on the topic they point out the guidance responsibilities of the school administrator, teacher, counselor, psychologist, supervisor of attendance, supervisor of instruction, curriculum consultant, doctor, and nurse.[14] Together these specialists seek to accomplish the school's objectives and the aims of a guidance program.

The other view contends that in the elementary schools, guidance and teaching are synonymous. In its extreme form, this point of view claims that all elementary school teachers are guidance specialists and daily performing guidance functions inseparable from teaching. This teacher-guidance relationship is supported by Willey who emphasizes that "guidance in elementary education cannot be regarded as an innovation because it is synonymous with teaching." [15] Those who espouse this view generally recognize a need for

---

[13] Harold F. Cottingham, *Guidance in Elementary Schools: Principles and Practices* (Bloomington, Illinois: McKnight and McKnight Publishing Company, 1956), p. 2.

[14] *Guidance in the Elementary School*, California State Department of Education Bulletin, Vol. XXIII, No. 4 (August, 1954), 8.

[15] Roy D. Willey, *Guidance in Elementary Education* (New York: Harper and Row, Publishers, 1952), p. 34.

specialists to handle the more serious cases but they are inclined not to identify this as a guidance function. They consider the chief guidance functionary in the elementary school to be the teacher, who works with children who have problems as a normal part of his teaching duties and helps to provide a classroom environment that is conducive to developing adjusted personalities as well as subject matter competence.

Two very prominent organizations, the National Association of Elementary School Principals [16] and the Association for Supervision and Curriculum Development, have devoted yearbooks to guidance and in support of the principal's and teacher's role. The ASCD, commenting on the role of the teacher, states:

> The instructional program is sufficiently flexible to enable the teachers to make substantial adjustments in it, the better to meet the needs of each of their pupils. A teacher has the dual role of making these necessary adjustments in the instructional program and of helping pupils adjust themselves to those of its aspects which societal need renders less flexible. Classroom teaching is inseparable from guidance; the teacher guides as well as teaches.[17]

There is some evidence that the "services and specialists" approach is gaining in strength. Counselors are being employed to work in elementary schools, and specific guidance services at that level are becoming more common. Texts and articles on elementary school guidance topics, the majority of which directly or indirectly support this point of view, are appearing in increasing numbers. There is also a movement in elementary education toward requiring a higher degree of specialization of staff members, and an increase in efforts to free the teacher from noninstructional responsibilities to concentrate on the job of teaching.

Certification for counselors to work in elementary schools is also undergoing changes. At present only a few states (New Jersey, Texas, Wyoming) certificate counselors for elementary schools; yet many indicate that the counselor certificate can be validated for different grade levels. This indicates that although most states have not recognized a specific role for an elementary school counselor,

[16] *Guidance for Today's Children,* National Elementary School Principals Association Bulletin, Vol. XXXIV, No. 1 (September, 1954).

[17] *Guidance in the Curriculum,* Yearbook for the Association for Supervision and Curriculum Development (New York: National Education Association, 1955), p. 5.

there is a tendency to allow for some additional preparation so that counselors can perform at this level.

The present status of guidance in elementary education is somewhat unclear. There seems to be no question about whether or not it is needed; controversies arise only around the question of its meaning and implementation. Some favor specific services with specialists; others believe that guidance is the teacher's responsibility and inseparable from instruction. The former point of view seems to be fostered in the main by people in the field of pupil personnel work, particularly those in counselor education; the latter seems to have its primary strength in teachers, elementary school principals, and those who are concerned with the supervision of instruction in elementary education.

# CHAPTER VII

# School Psychological Services

Of the many functions of pupil personnel, school psychological services clearly relate most directly to that of insuring conditions conducive to optimum pupil development. In order to provide for all children, school staffs must include specialists who understand the educational and psychological needs of children who are physically and mentally handicapped, educationally retarded, or emotionally disturbed. Approximately 10 per cent of the pupil population in any school district will belong to one of these categories and will need special education provisions in order to benefit fully in the school program.[1] School psychological services were originally intended to aid teachers and school administrators in handling the problems presented by such children.

Today, although still very much concerned with the needs of the exceptional child, psychological services are much broader in scope and include provisions for all pupils. Using the knowledge and skill gained in training programs which emphasize the measurement of human behavior, human growth, and development, learning theory and principles, and the significance of individual differences, school psychologists work to improve the effectiveness of the total school program. During the last decade a variety of studies were conducted in which practicing school psychologists were questioned about their proper role. They rather consistently responded that the diagnostic case study involving individual testing was their major responsibility. Separate investigations in California[2] and Ohio,[3] as well as a nationwide study conducted by the American

---

[1] Lloyd M. Dunn, "The Exceptional Pupil—A Challenge to Secondary Education," *The Education of Handicapped and Gifted Pupils in the Secondary School,* National Association of Secondary-School Principals Bulletin, Vol. 39, No. 202 (January, 1955), 9.

[2] Eli Michael Bower, *The School Psychologist,* California State Department of Education Bulletin, Vol. XXIV, No. 12 (November, 1955), 1.

[3] Donald G. Ferguson, "Duties, Training, and Certification of Ohio School Psychologists" (Doctoral dissertation presented at Western Reserve University, June, 1956), p. 74.

Psychological Association, showed remarkable consistency in this connection.[4] Other services which were frequently mentioned and which typically occurred in local programs include group testing, in-service education, special education, and research.

As school psychological services broaden, increasing attention is being given to the need to provide in the schools a healthy social and emotional climate for teachers and children alike. Emphasis, although still primarily focused on the intellectual development of children, now includes their total environment and their overall adjustment. Within this framework children are helped to adjust to their limitations—physical, mental, and emotional—and teachers are helped to adjust their expectations to these characteristics. School psychological services are now more than merely diagnostic services for children with limitations and deficiencies; they have broadened to include remedial and re-educative therapy in the emotional adjustment area as well as in the child's academic work.[5]

Changes in psychological services over the years have been accompanied by differences in opinion about what should constitute these services. As programs increase in number and broaden in scope, many school psychologists have come to believe that their services should be diagnostically-oriented and less concerned with the treatment of problems, at least until there are more competent specialists. Others believe that school psychologists must move beyond diagnostic activities and emphasize treatment and therapy. Still others believe school psychologists serve best as special consultants to teachers, administrators, and the board of education concerning questions of mental health.

### Individual Psychological Case Study

School psychologists typically spend 50 per cent or more of their time conducting evaluative studies of children who have been referred to them by the teacher or the principal. The children referred are for some reason displaying unadjustive behavior in the class-

---

[4] Norma Cutts, ed., *School Psychologists at Mid-Century* (Washington, D.C.: American Psychological Association, Inc., 1955), p. 32.

[5] T. Ernest Newland, "Psychological Services—Elementary and Secondary," *Encyclopedia of Educational Research,* 3rd ed. (New York: The Macmillan Company, 1960), p. 1068.

room. The problems range from difficulty with school subjects to behavior problems.

When a problem has been identified and referred to the school psychologist, on the basis of his background in personality theory and his clinical experience he forms an hypothesis as to what is causing the problem. The information he collects through testing and other techniques allows him to check the soundness of his hypothesis and to accept, modify, or reject it as other data indicate. When his hypothesis is confirmed, he is in a position to plan and recommend to the teacher steps which can be taken to help the individual. The final step is a follow-up procedure which provides an evaluation of the effectiveness of the diagnostic study and of the recommendations which were made.[6]

For example, an eight-year-old boy in the second grade appears to be unable to participate in the reading program and displays an unusual amount of aggressive behavior and hostility toward other children and at times toward the teacher as well. A referral to the school psychologist results in a mental examination revealing that, although the child is eight years of age, his mental development more closely approximates that of a six-year-old first grade child. The teacher should not hope and cannot expect to be successful with this boy beyond a first grade level of reading instruction. The psychologist's study shows a relationship between the child's aggressiveness and his fear and frustration because he was not able to compete with the other children in his second grade class.

In case study work the psychologist, working closely with the teacher, formulates a description of what the problem is, attempts to uncover its causes, and formulates a program for the child with a view toward more fully meeting his needs.

Very close relationship exists between a child's performance in school subjects and his social and emotional behavior. Although at times the causes underlying the instructional difficulty are in the emotional and social area, the reverse is frequently true. In the case just described, the youngster's inability to perform successfully in the school program caused behavioral difficulties. The teacher and the psychologist usually work together to modify the instruc-

---

[6] Eli Michael Bower, *The School Psychologist*, California State Department of Education Bulletin, Vol. XXIV, No. 12 (November, 1955), 10–14.

tional program to further both the child's behavioral adjustment and his academic work. In still other instances children referred for psychological evaluation are having school difficulties for which the cause is physical. Cases of this sort usually require that the school psychologists involve other specialists from pupil personnel, such as the school nurse, or that he work with the parents in referring the child for private or agency help.

A great variety of problems are referred to school psychologists in a typical school year. One state-wide study showed the number of children seen by each of 119 school psychologists to range from a low of 50 to a high of over 1,000 cases per year.[7] A reasonable estimate seems to be that a typical full-time school psychologist conducts about 300 studies a year.

## Group Testing

The responsibility of school psychologists to do group testing is less clear-cut. In some instances the school psychologist has complete authority for developing a district-wide group testing program; in others his duties in this respect are small.

Often the school psychologist's responsibility is one of coordination and consulting. He works with teachers of various grades and subjects to clarify which of their measurement questions are best answered by group-administered tests. Experience has shown that many of the school's evaluation questions can be answered by carefully selected and administered group tests. Group tests constitute the school's principal source of information about pupil aptitude for school work and pupil achievement in most subject areas. Group test results are also frequently used to diagnose strengths and weaknesses in the curriculum, and to discover specific educational needs of children from kindergarten through twelfth grade.

These testing instruments, like other tools of the teaching profession, have some very real limitations. Many measurement problems are not appropriately studied through a standardized group administered test, but through individually administered or teacher-

---

[7] Hazel C. McIntire, *A Survey of School Psychological Services in Ohio* (Columbus, Ohio: State Board of Education, 1959), p. 4.

made tests. Additional limitations relate to factors within the tests themselves and to external factors of test administration and scoring. More and more school systems are recognizing the need for specialists to help select from among the hundreds of achievement, intelligence, personality, aptitude, and other evaluative tests available today those which will best fit the needs of the particular school and class.

If the school psychologist has full responsibility for organizing and operating the group testing program, he must devote a great deal of his time and energy to carrying out this aspect of his job effectively. The American Psychological Association Committee on the Functions of School Psychology published a report which details the specific tasks which are involved:

1. Recommend testing programs and specific tests to meet needs of the system, a school, or an individual class.

2. Assist in preparation of test calendars and bulletins regarding group testing.

3. Supervise or consult on the group testing throughout the system, including achievement, intelligence, personality, aptitude, and other tests and evaluative instruments.

4. Demonstrate administration, interpretation, and use of group tests when they are first introduced, or for new staff members.

5. Administer group tests for purposes of pilot study or for demonstration, or when research demands specifically controlled testing procedures.

6. Train teachers to administer, interpret, and evaluate group tests; also administrators and counselors as required in a local situation.

7. Assist in evaluating the results of tests, measurements, sociograms, mental health surveys, etc., which may be administered by counselors, social workers, classroom teachers, or others.

8. Call attention to individuals whose group intelligence test results indicate need for follow-up, retesting, special classroom attention, or specialized referrals.

9. Supervise clerical assistants who
   a. Maintain a test file, and file of test publishers, distributors, and samples.
   b. Order, distribute, and maintain a perpetual inventory of test booklets, samples, manuals, and scoring keys.
   c. Account for all tests purchased and distributed.
   d. File all tests booklets after scoring.

e. Score group tests, calculate IQ's and other derived scores (secure machine where practical).

f. Type reports and interpretations of group testing.[8]

## In-Service Education

Many school psychologists believe that one of their chief contributions comes through working with teachers on in-service or staff development projects. In discussions with teachers, the school psychologist attempts to increase understandings and skills in areas such as the use of measurement instruments and techniques, the application of principles of human growth and individual differences, the principles of learning as related to good instruction and mental hygiene practices, and interviewing and conference techniques. In some school systems workshops and courses on these topics are conducted by school psychologists as a regular part of their services. A school psychologist in a medium-sized midwestern city, for example, spent two hours a week for an entire school year working with a group of elementary teachers and principals conducting an organized course in child mental hygiene. In this instance the participants were all employees of the local board of education who expressed a desire for some help on this mental health topic.

School psychologists also carry out staff development activities with individual teachers. The psychologist may spend as much time with a referring teacher as with the referred pupil, clarifying and interpreting information and helping the teacher in his perceptions about developmental and growth problems of children.

## Special Education

School psychologists have always had a major concern for special education. Their chief duties in this area are identifying and evaluating children who need placement in special classes. The school psychologist must be able to select and use evaluative techniques that fit the kind of disability being investigated. There are literally hundreds of tests from which to choose, some intended for specific

---

[8] *The Psychologists on the School Staff,* A Report of the Committee of Reconsideration of Functions of the School Psychologists, Division 16 (Washington, D.C.: American Psychological Association, October, 1958), pp. 12–13.

disabilities, some which are valid only for certain ages, and others which are more general. For evaluating mentally retarded children, for example, the tests—whether of intelligence, achievement, or whatever—must be so designed as to allow the child to demonstrate the extent of his ability.[9] Evaluation of blind and deaf children often requires a complicated set of skills. In addition to selecting appropriate appraisal devices for determining the child's school ability, psychologists must be able to weigh a host of factors related to the disability and to the proper placement of the child in the school program—the extent and the quality of language development, the identification of other sensory capacities for learning, and emotional and social strengths and needs.

The competent school psychologist will probably also be called upon for consultation on curriculum matters. In smaller school districts it is common practice for the school psychologist to direct the special education program—meeting with teachers, developing curriculum, recommending new classes, and arranging for pupil placements.

## Research

Although research is not considered a primary duty of school psychologists, it is one area in which they are expected to contribute and in which many school psychologists would like to be more active. A well-trained school psychologist has the ability to design research studies, to adapt and even to develop test instruments, to analyze research findings through a knowledge of statistics, and to interpret research findings. Through evaluative and testing procedures he can identify and isolate factors that would contribute to better instruction.[10]

As school psychologists' competencies in research become more clearly recognized, they are being called upon for a variety of contributions involving the application of statistics and research methodology to educational questions and problems. New and experimental instructional programs, such as the development of

---

[9] R. J. Capabianco, "Psychological Services in Special Education," *Education,* Vol. 77, No. 8 (April, 1957), 481.

[10] J. Wayne Wrightstone, "Research in School Psychology," in *Professional School Psychology,* eds. Monroe G. Gottsegen and Gloria B. Gottsegen (New York: Grune and Stratton, 1960), p. 265.

special provisions for children with learning problems, are an example of the kinds of research activities which are demanding more of the psychologist's time and energy. Numerous school systems during the last several years have attempted new kinds of programs for those children who have difficulty translating what they see or hear into meaningful and understandable associations and perceptions. Often, the cause is a defect in neurological development, and special instructional provisions are required. The school psychologist plays an important role not only in identifying and evaluating these children but also in designing experimental instructional programs and special studies to measure the effects of the instructional programs. This and many other examples of the school psychologist's involvement in research are appearing with increasing frequency.

## Professional Developments

The present scene in school psychology shows considerable variety. Although the psychologists have proved their worth and the number of new programs being initiated is steadily increasing each year, these services exist in less than half of the nation's school systems. To some extent, this is due to the relative newness of the services and to a lack of understanding by school administrators of both the nature of school psychological services and their value when weighed against questions of expense.

Another factor which has slowed the development of school psychological services has been that only recently has any professional organization provided leadership to clarify questions of role, training, and state certification. In 1948, the American Psychological Association became active and is currently striving to establish uniform patterns and standards throughout the nation. It is attempting to clarify the field and to upgrade school psychology on a national scale. A 1960 study showed that 23 states and the District of Columbia certificate school psychologists.[11] An increase over previous studies was indicated, yet more than half of the states still do not certificate these specialists for employment by the schools. The growth, although encouraging, has hardly been impressive.

[11] Walter L. Hodges, "State Certification of School Psychologists," *The American Psychologist,* Vol. 15, No. 6 (June, 1960), 346.

The number of employed school psychologists and the demand for them reflects the same sporadic growth. A study of 18 states indicated that at present approximately 2,500 certified school psychologists are working in the United States, with California employing an estimated 800; New York about 600; New Jersey about 200; Ohio about 170; and Michigan and Massachusetts approximately 150 each.[12] It is interesting to note that the respondents to the inquiry for the most part commented that there is a definite need as well as demand for more well-prepared specialists to work in this area of pupil personnel. A few states indicated a need but little demand since many school districts have not established budgets for developing these services.

---

[12] These estimates were obtained through correspondence with the following officials: (California) H. S. Morgan, Supervising Credentials Technician, Department of Education; (New York) William A. Sivers, Jr., Chief, Bureau of Psychological Services, the University of the State of New York; (New Jersey) J. Kirk Seaton, Director of Psychological Services, Department of Education; (Ohio) S. J. Bonham, Jr., Chief Psychologist, State Department of Education; (Michigan) Esther L. Belcher, Consultant, Department of Public Instruction; (Massachusetts) Nicholas J. Wells, Senior Supervisor, Division Special Education, Department of Education.

# CHAPTER VIII

# School Social Work Services

School social work is one of the oldest pupil personnel services. Although the job title—"school social worker"—appeared just recently, its predecessors, the attendance officer and the visiting teacher, have been in the schools much longer. Today these three specialists overlap in some of their activities, but distinctions are becoming clearer.

Attendance officers, the first of the home-visiting specialists to appear, are concerned principally with problems of nonattendance. Their methods are chiefly legalistic and authoritarian. Often their training and experience have been outside the school setting and include little professional preparation. Many, for example, are probation officers of the court assigned to the schools to do attendance work.

Visiting teachers appeared much later, and although they work with many of the same kinds of problems, they do so through an essentially nonauthoritarian approach. Rather than enforce compliance with the law, they try to help pupils and parents understand their legal obligation and also to appreciate the value of regular attendance. The visiting teacher's chief aim is to prevent attendance problems from becoming acute. His training and background usually include academic coursework and experience in teaching as well as some training in social work.

School social workers go even further in this approach to problems of nonattendance. Also, their scope of activities encompasses more than the prevention and correction of attendance problems. The training and experience of school social workers vary, of course, but major emphasis is usually placed on social case work philosophy and skills.[1]

---

[1] In this discussion the term "school social worker" will be used to refer to both the social worker and the visiting teacher. The title "visiting teacher" will be used only in quoting from other material.

## The Program of School Social Work Services

Like many of the other pupil personnel services, school social work focuses on the individual child and is essentially problem-centered: "The individual child naturally becomes a prime focus in a service which was established to help children whose problems stem from social and emotional causes that interfere with the school's program for achieving its educational objectives." [2]

School social workers strive to facilitate the work of teachers and principals, and often work directly with parents as well as children. Their major concern is with the school child who, because of behavior or attitude, is a problem to himself and others. The child's difficulty may be expressed through an inability to adjust to attendance requirements, an inability to complete school assignments, general misbehavior, or a host of other social and emotional symptoms which—although more difficult to discern—are no less indicative of a need for assistance. The underlying causes usually involve the child's family relationships or his relationships with other children and adults.

Several states which certificate specialists for employment in this field have described their roles in specially prepared bulletins. A Connecticut bulletin states: "The school social worker is a member of the school staff with specialized training for helping the child when something is interfering with his learning and growth, academically, socially, or emotionally." [3]

Pointing out that ". . . every child shall have an opportunity to benefit from school experience," [4] the Virginia State Board of Education certificates visiting teachers to assist classroom teachers, administrators and parents, and to work directly with pupils. "This service consists of helping . . . to discover and remove the causes of children's problems which result in irregular attendance, dislike for school, maladjustment and inability to succeed."

A similar statement by the California State Department of Edu-

---

[2] Francis C. Rosecrance and Velma D. Hayden, *School Guidance and Personnel Services* (Boston: Allyn and Bacon, Inc., 1960), p. 140.

[3] *The Team Approach in Pupil Personnel Services,* A Report by the Advisory Pupil Personnel Committee Dealing with the Role of School Social Workers, School Psychologists and School Counselors, Connecticut State Department of Education Bulletin 69 (Hartford, Conn., June, 1958), p. 12.

[4] *Visiting Teacher in Virginia's Program of Education,* Virginia State Board of Education Bulletin, Vol. XXXVIII, No. 13 (June, 1956), 3–4.

cation [5] emphasizes the social case work competence required in this activity. Through the application of case work skills the school social worker helps "individual children with emotional conflicts which are interfering with their development and their use of the school. . . ." The California bulletin emphasizes that in addition to helping children the case work method increases ". . . the value of the work of the classroom teacher."

Current school social work programs encompass a variety of functions and services, as do most areas of pupil personnel specialization. An analysis of these programs indicates three major functions: (1) evaluation and diagnosis in child-adjustment cases; (2) treatment in these cases; and (3) liaison between the school, the family, and community agencies.

*Evaluation of pupil adjustment cases.* A school social worker, when working with a disturbed child, attempts to clarify the nature of the problem and to recommend what realistically might be done to help. His major areas of competence, like those of the school psychologist, lie in diagnosis and evaluation. He investigates factors of a social, emotional, and educational nature concerning the child, the parents, and the home. This information, combined with that contributed by the teacher, principal, school counselor, school psychologist, and other school personnel, aids in the diagnostic process and emphasizes the way in which the school social worker serves as a team member in pupil personnel. The social worker provides insights into the relationship between the pupil's adjustment difficulty and his home situation, community and neighborhood factors, and other essentially nonschool environmental and interpersonal influences.

Interpersonal difficulties experienced outside of the school can be the direct or indirect cause of problems demonstrated by children in the classroom. Parents, money problems or marital difficulties may affect the child; the appearance of a new baby in the family might leave him insecure in his position. If the child lives in a home which lacks respect for education and does not provide motivation for learning, the child may perform at a level far below what his teachers believe should be expected of him in terms of his grade level and his abilities. It has long been an established fact that

---

[5] *The Preparation and Training of Pupil Personnel Workers,* California State Department of Education Bulletin, Vol. XXI, No. 5 (April, 1952), 27.

teachers face a virtually impossible task in trying to reach the child who is not motivated to learn as a result of earlier training by his parents. On the other hand, unrealistic parental aspiration may force a child to work beyond his ability level. Here symptoms of pressure may be demonstrated in undisciplined school behavior. In all of these and a variety of other such problems, a diagnosis is necessary to show the relationship between the symptoms which are being exhibited in school and their causes.

*Treating the child and the parent.* The second major function which many school social workers perform is treating a disturbed child with the objective of lessening his problem and increasing his chances for a fruitful school experience. "Social case work" is the term usually applied to this phase of school social work, and the principal activity is the case work interview. Case work is generally described as a method of treatment and is similar to, although not identical with, methods used by other members of the pupil personnel team. Through a series of interviews with the child or perhaps his parents, and through a knowledge of the child's personality, developmental history, life experiences, and his capacities for learning ". . . the school social worker attempts to interpret, and to utilize all the forces that will help the child to make a better personal, social, and school adjustment." [6]

Working directly with the child, the school social worker's objective is to help him recognize, clarify, verbalize, and more adequately handle feelings and attitudes that have developed in connection with the problem as it is uncovered through case study. Such help will often aid the pupil to a better understanding of those negative feelings which may be denying him the effective use of his capacities for successful participation in the school's activities. Typical of such help is a case reported by a school social worker whose 10-year old client felt rejected at home and who transferred the hostility she felt toward her family to her teachers and classmates. Through a series of interviews the social worker was able to help this girl see her home situation somewhat more realistically. She was eventually helped to understand why she felt and behaved as she did and consequently was able to handle her feelings better.

A school social worker's case activities can be divided into four

---

[6] *The Team Approach in Pupil Personnel Services,* p. 12.

kinds with varying degrees of intensity as discussed in Rosecrance and Hayden: [7] (1) intensive; seeing the child is seen on a regular basis; (2) consultative; working with teachers and other school personnel on the child's behalf; (3) cooperative; sharing the case with a community agency worker; and (4) supportive; seeing the child from time to time to support him in his school adjustment.

If the child's school problem is directly related to his interpersonal relationships with his father and mother or the home setting, the school social worker will often work with the parents. The social worker might conduct a series of interviews with the parents which are intended to aid in the diagnostic study but which are also clearly treatment-centered. Great skill and clarity of purpose are required if the school social worker is to function properly and effectively in this role. Interest must be shown in the parents and their problems so that they will feel secure and be able to talk through some of their feelings and concerns. At the same time, however, the social worker must make clear that his purpose is to bring about a more satisfactory adjustment for the child in the school program. The parents must be made to understand that the social worker's purpose is not to pry into their private lives nor to provide personal counseling other than as part of the school's effort to provide for their child's best development. Generally, the social worker will not allow his treatment interviews with parents to go into great depth or to be conducted over a long period of time. His objective is to help the parents identify and clarify their feelings and attitudes and, if necessary, seek help from some private or community counseling agency.

The effectiveness of the social worker in his work with teachers depends on many factors. In working with a teacher who has referred a child, for example, the social worker must respect the fact that he is working with a professional person. He must recognize that teachers too have certain unique skills and competence to be used in bringing about a better adjustment of the child, and that they generally are major contributors to any treatment. There must be an attempt to understand the referred problem as the teacher feels it and from his point of view. Teachers seldom see a child in the same light as the social worker. The child acts differently as

---

[7] Francis C. Rosecrance and Velma D. Hayden, *School Guidance and Personnel Services,* pp. 144–45.

one in a group of thirty than he does as an individual and not under group influence; yet, at times, the teacher might be over-reacting or inappropriately reacting to the child's behavior. Also, the teacher's involvement with the child is apt to be close and personal and less objective than that of a pupil personnel specialist. In such instances, the teacher's attitudes and behavior may need to be altered in order to effect a favorable learning climate for the pupil. The social worker might see the child as a member of a family or as a member of a class in school; but he must translate his perceptions and findings in such a way that they will be meaningful to the teacher. They must lead to some practical suggestion in terms of the limitations within which the teacher must work with the child. Regardless of the difficulty involved, in order to treat the child effectively, the social worker must also aid the teacher in his work and relationship with the child.

*Liaison between school and community.* A third major responsibility of the school social worker is to establish and maintain cooperation and good working relationships between the school and community agencies. The modern American community has an active group of child welfare and mental health agencies which, if used properly, supplement the pupil personnel program. Some examples are the child welfare agency, community guidance center, Family Service Association, Neighborhood House, and Catholic Social Services. These typically employ social work and psychological specialists similar to those found on a pupil personnel team. Many are clinical agencies employing psychiatrists, as well as other specialists, to do diagnostic work and to do intensive treatment which generally the school cannot do. Experience has also shown that the influence of these agencies is effectively brought to bear on school problems only if someone in the school takes responsibility to relate the efforts of the two institutions and provide coordination.

Other resources in the community also aid the efforts of pupil personnel where coordination is provided. Some of these are medical and psychological specialists in private practice and institutions such as churches, courts, and even the community library.

The school social worker, as a liaison specialist, helps the school and the agencies to communicate more effectively with one another so that there can be the fullest cooperation possible with a minimum of duplication of effort. He interprets the school to the agencies and the agencies to the school and can point out to each where unnecessary duplication and vital gaps in services exist.

## Professional Developments

Certification and training in this area of pupil personnel specialization have not developed as rapidly as one might expect. According to a study by Armstrong and Stinnett [8] in 1959, only 16 states issue credentials in this field, 4 in school social work and 12 for visiting teachers.

Similarly, training institutions have been slow in developing programs to prepare these specialists for school employment. Training patterns appear to be of two kinds, each of which is more properly described as retraining. In one, a classroom teacher may take additional course credit in social case work. The second provides for professional preparation in a school of social work after which the person usually must complete the requirements necessary for teacher certification. Neither of these is entirely satisfactory, which points up the need for specific attention to training as one of the most critical professional problems facing school social workers.

---

[8] W. Earl Armstrong and T. M. Stinnett, *A Manual on Certification Requirements for School Personnel in the United States* (Washington, D.C.: National Education Association, 1959).

# CHAPTER IX

# Child Accounting
# and Attendance Services

The oldest existing services in pupil personnel work are those of child accounting and attendance. In the late 1800's the first compulsory school attendance legislation made it necessary for school districts to identify the children who were eligible to attend school and to see that they came to school on a regular basis. Even today school systems exist in which the only pupil personnel service offered is in this area.

Child accounting and attendance are very closely related aspects of the same general responsibility. Yet each is geared to specific purposes; and each involves different operations, methods, and —generally—different workers. Throughout the years the essential responsibilities of these services have remained rather stable, as is pointed out by Culbertson:

> Although the goals of attendance administration in many countries have shifted from legal enforcement to the broader concept of providing attendance services, its basic tasks have remained unchanged. Aiding in the enforcement of compulsory attendance laws, maintaining an adequate school census and enrollment and attendance records, and studying factors related to and affecting attendance are its major tasks.[1]

Specifically, two major tasks are assigned to this aspect of personnel work: (1) locating the children of school age who reside within the district and (2) keeping them in school under the conditions specified in the attendance laws. The first is essentially a job of child accounting and includes taking the school census. The second involves work with teachers, principals, parents, and other pupil personnel workers, and the pupils themselves to insure the regular attendance of each child in the district.

---

[1] Jack Culbertson, "Attendance," *Encyclopedia of Educational Research*, 3rd ed. (New York: The Macmillan Company, 1960), p. 92.

## Child Accounting

Procedures for child accounting in most states are made mandatory by state legislatures in connection with compulsory school attendance laws. The value of an education is a basic American belief. The security of our nation and the preservation of our way of life requires an informed and participating citizenry. Out of this belief has developed a universal educational system designed to insure that each child receives an education commensurate with his ability. To insure this it is necessary first to identify all children who are of legal school age. Throughout the nation school districts accomplish this primarily through an annual enumeration and the maintenance of a continuous census record. Although child accounting is generally viewed as encompassing more than simply enumeration and census, these constitute its core activities.

Child accounting must answer several questions and these have remained fairly stable over the last few decades. A school district needs accurate and up-to-date information about the number of children living in the district who are of school age, the number who live in the areas served by specific buildings within the district, the age and grade status of all pupils, the whereabouts of those children of the district who are enrolled in a private or parochial school, and the status of children of school age who are not attending any school.[2] Child accounting, therefore, is essentially an administrative job, and it is an important vehicle through which pupil personnel services facilitate the efforts of school administrators. Originally the major purpose of the school census was administrative rather than child-centered: it provided a basis on which to distribute state funds for the support of local schools. Without the benefit of accurate census data, school administrators would be unable to plan for the teacher personnel, equipment, and the physical plant needs necessary to provide an adequate program of education. Morphet, Johns, and Reller cite several problems faced by school administrators for which an accurate annual estimate of the student population is required.

The administration has to know how many pupils will have to be housed in each school, and any shifts of population that are

---

[2] Arch O. Heck, *Administration of Pupil Personnel* (Boston: Ginn and Company, 1929), p. 143.

occurring in each district. Any construction program in the district is apt to present an additional problem of supplying temporary quarters for classes for the children of new families. Boundaries of school districts cannot be changed until school population figures are known. Provisions for transportation to school and the details of routing, employment of bus drivers, and special provision for the handicapped depend on estimates from census data.

Census figures are also important in determining the number of teachers needed for a given year and in planning the school budget. Census information is necessary in estimating the material—tests, instructional material, supplies—that will be needed for the school year and for planning class schedules.[3]

Facts collected in census studies vary among the states and among the communities in any given state. According to Umbeck:

> At present it is mandatory in 43 states that a school census be taken . . . . The age span, the frequency of enumeration, and the period of the year during which the census is taken, differed in the various states. The most popular age spans are 0 to 18 (8 states); 6 to 21 (8 states); and 6 to 18 (7 states).[4]

Methods for taking the school census vary. In school systems where there are organized departments of pupil personnel, the assignment for devising an effective and efficient census program is usually given to the director of the department. He then must select from among many possible methods one which will most adequately do the job in his particular district. Paid interviewers are employed in some districts; in others, teachers make a house-to-house canvass. It is not uncommon for the director or an assistant director to program a year-around enumeration system which requires only a clerical staff to collect information and keep records.

The chief aim of the child accounting and attendance program within pupil personnel, therefore, is to identify the children of the school district who are eligible and, in fact, obligated to attend school. The chief vehicle through which this is accomplished is

[3] Edgar L. Morphet, R. L. Johns, and Theodore L. Reller, *Educational Administration: Concepts, Practices, and Issues* (Englewood Cliffs, N.J.: Prentice-Hall, Inc., 1959), pp. 372–73.

[4] Nelda Umbeck, *State Legislation on School Attendance and Related Matters— School Census and Child Labor,* U.S. Department of Health, Education, and Welfare Circular No. 573 (Washington, D.C.: U.S. Office of Education, January 1, 1959), p. 7.

the school census or enumeration which, in addition to focusing attention on the individual child, provides a source of regular and continuous enrollment data essential for a variety of planning and program requirements.

## Attendance Work

Once the children of the school district have been located, the next important step is to keep them in school. This is the work of attendance personnel.

Attendance activities, like those in child accounting, are tied directly to state statutes. Since education in the United States is the legal responsibility of the state, each state determines its own specific requirements for school attendance. Similarly, each state decides where the responsibility for the enforcement of school attendance laws will be placed. Commonly this responsibility is delegated to local school districts. Seldom does the state itself establish an agency to carry out direct control over school attendance.

The approach in attendance work in American elementary and secondary schools has undergone considerable revision since its early beginnings. Originally, attendance work was almost entirely authoritarian and legalistic, placing great emphasis upon the police power of the. attendance officer. The aim was primarily to force children to attend school regularly; very little attention was paid to determining the causes of nonattendance or to considering the possibility of their alleviation. Attendance enforcement today does not simply involve force and compulsion. This shift of emphasis began with the development of the newer services in pupil personnel—school social work, school psychological services, and guidance.

One of the primary motivations underlying the development of the newer approach was the conviction of some educators that a more realistic attack on attendance problems should provide trained and skillful specialists to work with these children. Pointing out the shift in emphasis and the way in which new personnel were brought into the attendance effort is a bulletin by the Pennsylvania Department of Public Instruction which states:

> The fundamental purpose of the program has shifted with the changing philosophy of education. The way in which provisions of

the school laws are worked indicates quite clearly that according to the earlier conception of this particular function, home and school visitors were considered attendance officers. While this particular responsibility is not now ignored, the home and school visitor, acting in the light of special preparation and on the basis of an enlightened philosophy of education, is not only concerned with the fact of nonattendance or irregular attendance, and employment, but is also interested in the educational, psychological, medical, and social problems and needs of children who are attendance problems.[5]

The major agent in modern attendance work is the attendance officer who still retains police power and, who, for the most part, continues to operate in an authoritarian way through the exercise of that authority. In contrast to his predecessors, however, he is alert to the fact that attendance problems often are corrected more effectively if they are studied and treated as a symptom rather than as an isolated problem. Through such insight the attendance officer draws upon the services of the other pupil personnel members to investigate and cooperate in the formulation of a program of treatment and correction. For example, a boy in the seventh grade is having difficulty adjusting to a large junior high school. Like many children, this boy felt very secure in the rather protective elementary school but now feels very insecure in the larger, more impersonal junior high school. In reaction, he takes advantage of every opportunity to stay out of school, inventing excuses to make his absences appear reasonable. Recognizing the symptomatic nature of the behavior, the attendance officer seeks help from the school social worker and the school psychologist. Together, and with help from the teacher, they counsel with the boy and the adults involved, rather than punish him for breaking the rules.

It must be stressed, however, that despite this newer approach, the attendance officer is in essence an officer of the state who has certain specific responsibilities to discharge by way of implementing state laws. His duties are clearly pointed out by Umbeck who states:

> The duties of the attendance officer are to check on every child who is of compulsory school age in their jurisdiction to determine whether the child is either (1) attending public school; (2) receiv-

---

[5] *Manual for Child Accounting and Pupil Personnel Work in Pennsylvania*, Department of Public Instruction Bulletin 71, (Harrisburg, Pa.: Department of Public Instruction, 1953), p. 85.

ing instruction in a private or parochial school, or at home, where the instruction is substantially the equivalent of that given in the public school; or (3) exempt from compulsory school attendance in accordance with the laws of the state.[6]

In discharging these responsibilities it is often necessary for the attendance officer to exercise his police power. At times he must arrest children who are violating school attendance laws and represent the school in court action if such becomes necessary. From time to time it is necessary for him to enter places where children are employed to investigate whether or not they are legally absent from school and working under conditions which are within the limits prescribed by the law.

## The Specialist in Attendance Work

In the available literature dealing with this area of pupil personnel, reference is made not only to the attendance officer but also to the important role played by other specialists such as visiting teachers, home-school visitors, and social workers. Certainly, the vital role played by these specialists in effecting better pupil attendance or investigating nonattendance cases cannot be denied. It is important, however, to point out that within this broader concept of modern attendance work there continues to be a need for the more aggressive role of the attendance officer. Many, if not most, school systems would like to devote more time and effort to a thorough investigation of all cases of nonattendance; however, this is unrealistic at present and it will undoubtedly continue to be for some time to come.

One of the reasons why school systems have been employing newer specialists to aid in the attendance function is that over the period of years attendance officers have been the most poorly prepared and least professional of all of the specialists in pupil personnel. The lack of specific training and professional preparation for the role they perform continues even today as it did in 1949 when Yeager reported:

> Only 10 states have set up any educational qualifications for the office represented by some form of certification, usually state controlled. These qualifications include, for the most part, preparation

---

[6] Umbeck, *State Legislation on School Attendance,* p. 6.

in the teaching and social service fields and experience in teaching, or its equivalent.[7]

Even today in most states no qualifications are specified, and in many school districts all that is required is that applicants have graduated from high school. All too often these appointments have been political and without any regard to competencies necessary to do the job. It is reported that some attendance officers have previously been painters, electricians, meat cutters, and that others have come from a variety of occupational groups. In some instances they have been appointed on the strength of physical qualifications and a disposition that reflects roughness and toughness.

Attendance is one of the most important, yet least professionally performed, services. There has been progress, however. Initially the service provided was one of police power, but more recently attention has been focused on the reasons for nonattendance as well. Hopefully, with an increased awareness of the symptomatic nature of continuing absence, child accounting and attendance workers will strive for greater understanding through education and professionalization.

---

[7] Yeager, *Administration and the Pupil*, p. 76.

# CHAPTER X

# School Health Services

A modern school health program consists of three aspects: school health services, instruction in health and safety, and provisions for a safe and healthful environment. Authorities generally agree that these three aspects must be adequately provided and integrated into the school program if the aims of American elementary and secondary schools are to be accomplished. The earlier interpretation of the school health program which emphasized only the detection of communicable diseases and the exclusion and subsequent readmission of affected pupils is now regarded as too limited. Today disease control, although important, is viewed as merely one aspect of the overall program of health education and services.

Across the nation, schools are increasing their efforts to instruct pupils in health information and to help them develop good health habits. Also increasing are health services which the school provides to insure optimum pupil health and a healthful school environment.

## The Program of School Health Services

Health factors, more than any other cause, account for the largest amount of pupil nonattendance. Fifteen per cent of all pupils are absent daily, usually because of illness. Illness is also cited as the largest cause of nonpromotion.[1] A high relation exists between the incidence of physical defects and illness and poor scholastic achievement. Furthermore, if a child is not physically well, he will also have problems of adjustment in areas other than subject matter. Certainly there is agreement that if children are to profit from the school experience, they must be reasonably healthy and have benefit of school services which will attend to their well-being.

---

[1] Ward G. Reeder, *The Fundamentals of Public School Administration*, 4th ed. (New York: The Macmillan Company, 1958), pp. 433–34.

Throughout the history of education in America, pupil health has been a concern to educators and also to lawmakers. Every state has enacted statutory provisions both to protect and to improve the health of school pupils. The range of these provisions is broad, and often included are measures to insure that school buildings will not be built near institutions or situations presenting health hazards, set standards of lighting and ventilation, require programs of immunization and health examination, and the employment of medical specialists. Almost every state makes statutory provision for the employment of a school nurse and a school physician.[2]

There is considerable variation in the adequacy with which health services are provided. Some schools have developed well-coordinated programs employing a health service director, specially trained nurses, and full-time or consulting physicians and medical specialists. In other schools, however, attention to pupil health is given only through a few routine checks which teachers are required to make.

It is very doubtful that many, if any, schools actually have as many services or staff as are needed to conduct an optimum school health services program. Health services, like some other pupil personnel services, often put a heavy burden on the school budget. Boards of education which employ their own specialists often pay them from board funds without any substantial state financial support. This being the case, they may choose to get by with as little service as possible in order to not arouse the taxpayer. Health service is an area in which a board can economize by choosing not to employ its own specialists since these services often are available at little or no cost through a community health agency.

School health programs are organized in a variety of ways, but two broad patterns appear. The first is a cooperative agreement between a board of education and a community agency, such as the county board of health. Such arrangements emphasize the school's role as an important agency for community health particularly in the detection and control of contagious diseases. The schools benefit through these arrangements since, in addition to

---

2 Winston L. Roesch, *Statutory Basis for Administrative and Specialized Service Staffing in Local School Districts,* United States Department of Health, Education and Welfare Bulletin OE–23000, No. 1 (Washington, D.C.: U.S. Office of Education, 1960), pp. 42–48.

contributing to the broader community health effort, they receive certain medical services at limited expense or no expense to the board of education. Historically, these cooperative health services programs have been of considerable significance. Today, however, they are decreasing in number and appear mainly in those schools where, because of budget limitations or lack of available personnel, local boards of education have been reluctant to develop their own program.

The second common pattern in the organization of health services is one in which the board of education organizes its own program and employs its own specialists. As communities have grown more alert to their responsibilities for financing and providing an adequate program of education, health services have become directly attached to the board of education.

A study conducted by the American School Health Association reported that:

> . . . in 1950 a national survey revealed that in 91 per cent of cities with a population of 2,500 persons or more, some type of school health service was being provided. In 60 per cent of the cases, the board of education had sole administrative authority for the program while there was joint responsibility between boards of health and boards of education in 23 per cent of the cities studied. Thus, in 83 per cent of the cases, the board of education had all or at least a part of the responsibility for the school health program.[3]

In general, school officials believe that the most effective health services program is one which is board-operated. They claim that a broader and more comprehensive program of health education and services can be provided if responsibility for them is assumed by the school. Supporting this contention, Reeder [4] comments on several objections or shortcomings of the cooperative health service concepts. When community agencies are responsible, they tend to limit the program to the control of contagious diseases and other elements of the prevention program and ignore the educational aspects. The cooperative program also lacks the natural liaison between the school, the home, and other community agencies

---

[3] "The Report of the Committee on School Health Service Facilities of the American School Health Association," *The Journal of School Health,* Vol. XXVIII, No. 1 (January, 1958), 7.

[4] Reeder, *The Fundamentals of Public School Administration,* p. 438.

which is possible when the services are school-centered. Liaison in this regard is highly desirable since some of the most effective work in health is done by the classroom teacher and the school principal.

The literature abounds with discussions and definitions of school health programs. One very clear statement was formulated by a joint committee of the National Education Association and the American Medical Association in which a distinction is made between the three major aspects of a school health program:

> *School health services* are procedures established: (a) to appraise the health status of pupils and school personnel; (b) to counsel pupils, parents, and others concerning appraisal findings; (c) to encourage the correction of remediable defects; (d) to assist in the identification and education of handicapped children; (e) to help prevent and control disease; and (f) to provide emergency service for injury or sudden sickness.
>
> *School health education* is the process of providing learning experiences for the purpose of influencing knowledge, attitudes, or conduct relating to individual and community health.
>
> *Healthful school living* designates the provision of a safe and healthful environment, the organization of a healthful school day, and the establishment of interpersonal relationships favorable to emotional, social, and physical health.[5]

The modern school health services program operating as a vital part of the pupil personnel program emphasizes ". . . the student's total health potential."[6] The school health staff consults with parents, teachers, administrators and the students at times to achieve a better understanding of the child's health needs and at other times to arrange for adjustment in home and school provisions. Often physical needs as well as specific defects are uncovered early in the child's school program which can then be corrected before serious adjustment difficulties develop. Children whose visual or hearing deficiencies went undetected and untreated sometimes developed serious physical defects. Their school work suffered as a natural consequence, and they experienced difficulties in social and emotional adjustment too.

[5] Charles C. Wilson, ed., *School Health Services* (Washington, D.C.: National Education Association, 1953), pp. 5–6.

[6] Marie A. Hinrichs, "Health Services Elementary and Secondary," *Encyclopedia of Educational Research,* 3rd ed. (New York: The Macmillan Company, 1960), p. 641.

## The School Health Specialists

Today several different kinds of medical specialists work in the schools on either a regular or limited basis, and all school districts have at least one. Unquestionably, the major specialist among these is the school nurse, both from the point of view of the number employed and the importance of the work being done.

School nurses have been a part of elementary and secondary education in America for many years. Theirs has been a changing role and one of increasing necessity as schools have moved toward an emphasis on understanding children as prerequisite to effective teaching. The school nurse today has a broad and important job to perform. She must be able to organize and schedule a medical appraisal program, provide emergency care, contribute to the development of positive health attitudes and practices among pupils and staff, supervise a disease control program, contribute to the pupil personnel effort of identifying and planning for handicapped children, and serve as a resource person on health instruction questions and on questions of teacher health.[7]

The trend in school nursing, like that in other areas of pupil personnel specialization, appears to be in the direction of a specific set of responsibilities requiring competence in medical specialization and also carrying out important pupil personnel team responsibilities. In addition to organizing and operating school health programs of medical appraisal, emergency care, and the like, the school nurse must also participate as a member of a diagnostic team which includes the school psychologists, school social workers, teachers, and others. Similarly the modern school nurse contributes to the broader pupil personnel effort of advising administrators and committees of teachers on curriculum revision projects and other efforts which affect the school's total program of instruction and services. An example of a way in which the school nurse of today is participating in programs affecting large numbers of children and teachers is the pre-kindergarten or pre-first grade "round-up" program. These programs are becoming fairly common and typically involve several members of the pupil personnel staff as well as teachers and principals. During the "round-up," which

---

[7] Dorothy C. Tipple, "The Changing Role of the School Nurse," *Teachers College Record*, Vol. 59 (January, 1958), 191–95.

occurs in the spring or late summer preceding the beginning of school, an attempt is made to identify the children who will be entering kindergarten or the first grade during the coming year. Medical information, school ability, and related facts about the children are collected and analyzed, and the parents are informed of the nature and the requirements of the coming school experience. School nurses play an important role in this program for, in addition to checking for gross physical difficulties, they work with teachers to appraise the child's readiness for the activities and experiences of kindergarten. They help to spot children who, although old enough to attend kindergarten, might be physically immature or who, for some other reason or combination of reasons, will need to be carefully watched.

The exact number of nurses employed in the nation's schools is not known; however, a substantial growth in these services is reported. Every school system today has one or more medical specialists available either as an employee of the board of education, through the state board of education, or through a cooperative agreement with a local health agency. Byrd, in the *School Health Sourcebook* states: "During the period from 1937 to 1951 it is reported that the number of school nurses employed by boards of education increased from 3,477 to 6,088." [8]

Hagerman comments that although the largest percentage of registered nurses is employed by local health agencies, the next largest group—29 per cent—is employed by boards of education. This number, Hagerman reports, ". . . increased almost 13 per cent during the two-year period from 1953 to 1955, and has more than doubled since 1937, the first year in which data were tabulated by the United States Public Health Service." [9]

The training of school nurses varies from state to state as does certification. Generally, the belief among school nurses is that existing training programs and present state certification patterns are in need of revision, principally to make them more consistent with the specific jobs nurses must perform in schools. Indications are that school health officials are working vigorously to bring

---

[8] Oliver E. Byrd, *School Health Sourcebook* (Stanford, Calif.: Stanford University Press, 1955), p. 146.

[9] Lily C. Hagerman, "The 1955 Census of Public Health Nurses," *American Journal of Nursing*, Vol. 55, No. 12 (December, 1955), 1493–96.

about desirable changes and that some encouraging progress is evident. Dilworth,[10] for example, reports that studies of state laws about the certification and employment of nurses for school work indicate an awareness by state departments of education of the need for specific preparation for this task.

The school nurse certainly is a main strength of the medical and health services program in the schools. Even today in some school districts she works alone without other medical specialists to aid her. Increasingly, however, through a recognition of the need for competent and comprehensive school health services, boards of education are employing other medical specialists on a full- or part-time basis. Many modern school systems, for example, employ school physicians, dental specialists, otologists, and ophthalmologists.

School physicians have long been an important part of school health programs, and in recent years have been regarded as increasingly necessary to carry out the modern school health program effectively. The American Medical Association has been working continuously and effectively with the American Association of School Administrators in an attempt to provide guidelines for the participation of the physician in the school's health program and, at the same time, to increase the effectiveness of the school's participation in larger community health programs.

Evidence of the many ways in which school physicians contribute to the health services program is presented in a recent study of the American School Health Association which investigated the responsibilities of school physicians.[11] Ranked highest in importance by school physicians were their responsibilities in the broad areas of coordination of health and services, prevention of disease, consultations with other medical specialists on school health problems, and public relations. In addition to these broad categories 95 specific duties were listed and ranked in order of importance. High on the list were: working with school nurses, coordination of school health and public health programs implementing pupil exclusion and readmission policies for the control of communicable diseases,

---

[10] Lula P. Dilworth, "Study of Certification of School Nurses," *Journal of School Health,* Vol. XXVIII, No. 3 (March, 1958), 64.

[11] R. L. Bonvechio and D. A. Dukelow, "Responsibilities of School Physicians," *The Journal of School Health,* Vol. XXXI, No. 1 (January, 1961), 21–30.

consulting with school officials to develop all aspects of a school health program, developing and implementing policies for emergency care of illness and accident cases, developing and participating in immunization programs, and performing medical examinations of children referred by teachers or nurses for specific health reasons.

Indeed much has been done by school officials and by physicians themselves to improve both the quantity and quality of their participation in the school's health program. Startling evidence exists, however, that much needs to be accomplished before an effective integration of physicians into school health programs and pupil personnel programs can be realized. The respondents in the above-mentioned study, for example, rated in-service teacher education and special education among the least important of their responsibilities. These are areas which teachers and administrators generally consider to be important aspects of a school physician's program. Many feel, for example, that he should work with teachers by helping them to develop skill in identifying pupils with gross and subtle medical problems that might be affecting their participation in the school program. Similarly many believe that school physicians could serve more effectively if they worked more closely with teachers as consultants on medical and health aspects of the daily classroom program. These opinions are common, particularly among teachers of special education classes where the children generally have some special medical problems which require particular attention as part of the instructional program.

Another important area of medical specialization in the school health program is dental services. A recent study which involved over 3,000 elementary and secondary schools states that ". . . 3 out of every 5 schools (60.4%) provide some dental service for some of their children." [12] The most commonly provided service is the oral examination which typically is administered by the school dentist, the hygienist, or the school nurse. In almost all instances, where the examination indicates the need for treatment, referral is made either to the family dentist or to some community facility. The schools which provide dental treatment and care are in the minority.

With pupil personnel programs developing rapidly in American

---

[12] Melvin L. Dollar and Perry J. Sandell, "Dental Programs in Schools," *The Journal of School Health,* Vol. XXXI, No. 1 (January, 1961), 9.

elementary and secondary schools the importance of medical and health services is becoming more widely recognized. Several groups are at present actively working toward a clarification of the role of the services and the specialists with a view to bringing about a better integration of them in the overall school effort.

# CHAPTER XI

# Other Programs and Specialists

The services and specialists discussed thus far are quite clear-cut in terms of their placement in the pupil personnel classification of educational specialization. Others, though often included in pupil personnel, are not so clearly placed. For example, special education is an area which some educators claim lies more nearly in instructional services than in pupil personnel. Speech correction, audiology, and remedial instruction—like special education—are areas of specialization. The question is continuously raised: Are these more appropriately and effectively coordinated as pupil personnel or as instructional services?

A number of these services and specialists have been selected for discussion here. The focus is on the nature of these services and a few of their special characteristics, not on whether or not they more appropriately belong in pupil personnel or instruction.

Actually, is it questionable whether school organization and administration will ever be refined to the point of having a clear-cut delineation of the various services and responsibilities which fit into the three major areas—school administration, instruction, and pupil personnel. Hatch and Stefflre point out, ". . . no clear-cut distinction is always possible between the areas of instruction and of personnel services. There remains a twilight zone occupied by workers who are at once teachers of skills and at the same time largely involved in the adjustment of pupils." [1]

In this chapter mention is also made of school psychiatric services. There is no confusion about where these are most appropriately coordinated. Few schools have such services, yet they warrant attention because of indications that they will grow in importance as pupil personnel services develop.

---

[1] Raymond N. Hatch and Buford Stefflre, *Administration of Guidance Services: Organization, Supervision, Evaluation* (Englewood Cliffs, N.J.: Prentice-Hall, Inc., 1958), p. 110.

## Special Education

Special education is the adaptation of the school's program to pupils who are referred to as exceptional children. These are children who ". . . deviate from what is supposed to be the average in physical, mental, emotional, or social characteristics to such an extent that they require special educational services in order to develop to their maximum capacity." [2] Included in this category are children who are blind or partially sighted, deaf or hard of hearing, physically handicapped, emotionally or socially disturbed, and those who possess either exceptionally high intellectual endowment or are retarded in mental development. Estimates vary as to the number of exceptional children in any given population, but certainly in most school districts the number is large enough to require special attention.

The range of provisions for exceptional children varies among the states and also within any given state. In some school systems thorough diagnostic and instructional adaptation are made to insure both an early identification and a differentiated program of experiences. In others, virtually no special attention is given unless these pupils exhibit extreme deviations.

The most commonly adopted plan to provide for educational needs of exceptional children is the special class. In these an attempt is made to provide instruction similar to that received by other children but which contains the compensations required by the specific disability so that the child will have the same opportunity to profit from the school experience as other children.

Often special education is coordinated under pupil personnel services because identification and evaluation of these children is a prerequisite to the development of any instructional provision. In almost all instances where his services are available, the school psychologist will be an important person in the identification, diagnosis, and formulation of special teaching arrangements for these children. Similarly, the school social worker and the school nurse play an important role.

---

[2] Nelson B. Henry, ed., *The Education of Exceptional Children*, Forty-ninth Yearbook of the National Society for the Study of Education, Part II (Chicago, Ill.: The University of Chicago Press, 1950), p. 3.

## Speech Correction

A second major area of school activity which overlaps pupil personnel and instruction are the services provided for children with defective speech. Regardless of how these activities are coordinated in a school program, a great deal of the time of the speech correction specialist is spent in teaching language and conducting speech therapy, an activity usually thought of as a clerical service.

Authorities in the field of speech correction generally agree that the number of children with this handicap is quite large. According to one author, 12 to 15 per cent of the children through the fourth-grade level show serious speech defects. Among older pupils the number seems to decrease to about 4 to 5 per cent.[3]

The large number of children with speech defects is a major problem in our society and is a specific school problem. The question of which agency of society should accept the responsibility for rehabilitation of these individuals has long been raised. Contrary to the practice in other countries, responsibility in America has fallen mainly to the schools. "Our public-school system," Van Riper claims, "is about the only organization large enough to do the job. It can employ trained teachers and it has the child during those years when speech correction can be most effective."[4] The medical profession, which treats cases of speech defects in European countries, appears to be generally uninterested in these problems in this country.

Because educators have accepted responsibility for working with these children, speech correction has become a large area of special service in our schools and is one for which specialists are required. Some schools rely upon the classroom teacher to carry out the work necessary in correcting defective speech and to provide special instruction for children who have defective speech, but "the most efficient work is done by the special speech-correction teacher."[5]

---

[3] Robert Milisen, "The Incidence of Speech Disorders," in *Handbook of Speech Pathology,* ed. Lee E. Travis (New York: Appleton-Century-Crofts, Inc., 1957), p. 250.

[4] Charles Van Riper, *Speech Correction: Principles and Methods* (Englewood Cliffs, N.J.: Prentice-Hall, Inc., 1954), p. 11.

[5] *Ibid.,* p. 530.

## Audiology

A third special service, often very closely associated with speech correction, is audiology. In instances where a trained speech therapist is employed, that person often has had training in audiometric measurement and evaluation as well as in speech correction. Consequently he performs in both of these areas. The services of an audiologist in the school are employed mainly to identify and diagnose hearing loss or deafness in school children.

Concern today extends far beyond providing only for the approximately 1.5 per cent of pupils who are deaf or seriously hard of hearing. There are many youngsters whose hearing loss is not critical enough to warrant placement into special classes but who need to be identified early so that their difficulty can be recognized in the regular class. Allowances are made in the regular class to assure that they derive full benefit from the lessons.

The attention necessary to provide an adequate educational program for children with a hearing disability is an excellent example of the coordination which is necessary within pupil personnel services. It has been pointed out by Myklebust,[6] in his text on *The Psychology of Deafness,* that a relationship exists between deafness and social and emotional adjustment in both children and adults. This disability must be viewed in terms of its effect on the total personality.

## Remedial Instruction

A fourth area which requires attention is remedial work in the basic school subjects. Specialists in this area are involved in both pupil personnel and instruction. In some schools this service is often coordinated under pupil personnel services since much of the activity is clinical and diagnostic, emphasizing determining the causes of the difficulty before a decision is made about corrective measures. Most common of the specialists in this area are the reading diagnostician and the remedial reading teacher. Their attention is focused on school children who possess the intellectual capabilities for profiting in the instructional program but who have not demonstrated the expected level of achievement. The philosophy upon

---

[6] Helmer R. Myklebust, *The Psychology of Deafness: Sensory Deprivation, Learning, and Adjustment* (New York: Grune and Stratton, 1960), p. 77.

which remedial activities are based is that the abilities which are required to learn how to read and write are possessed by any child with normal intelligence. It follows then that any child with normal intelligence can learn these basic skills.[7]

Growing out of this philosophy there has developed in many school systems an extensive program of individual and small group remedial instruction. Clinical services have also been developed which aim to determine whether there is actually an inconsistency between the child's ability and his achievement or whether the estimates of his ability are inaccurate. In instances where analysis and diagnosis reveal that the child is truly capable of profiting, a program of specialized instruction is provided to narrow the gap between ability and performance.

## Psychiatric Services

School psychiatry is an example of a service which fits the rationale of pupil personnel but which is not a major speciality because of the scarcity of workers and programs. Psychiatrists are not commonly found in the school program, and exactly how they can be best employed in school work is not yet known. Hirning points out that although psychiatrists have rendered various services in some schools, their functions have never been clarified. Their employment may result from ". . . some purely personal association with a modern-minded school administrator who because the field is so new, brought the psychiatrist into the situation over the more or less silent skepticism of his colleagues." [8]

The background training and experience of school psychiatrists differ markedly from those of other specialists in the school. Consequently, their competencies are not clearly understood and their integration into the school program presents difficulties. Yet, where they have been employed, it is generally conceded that these services have made a strong contribution to the total pupil personnel effort. Fedder, speaking from experience (having worked on a staff where psychiatric services were available), discusses their role and also

---

[7] Grace M. Fernald, *Remedial Techniques in Basic School Subjects* (New York: McGraw-Hill Book Company, Inc., 1943), p. V.

[8] Clovis L. Hirning, "Functions of a School Psychiatrist," *Teachers College Record,* Vol. 59 (January, 1958), 211–24.

speaks of the time and patience needed to explore more fully how their services might be smoothly integrated into the school's program. From the point of view of the services they perform, she sees them as specialists in adjustment services who work with teachers and other specialists of the pupil personnel department ". . . to help develop educational procedures and an emotional climate which not only will prevent serious problems in some children but also will provide a better school experience for all children." [9]

She also mentions that they have a role as a consultant on the school's total mental health program and its program of early identification of problems.[10]

---

[9] Ruth Fedder, "Teacher and Psychiatrist Work Together," *Teachers College Record,* Vol. 61 (March, 1960), 340–41.

[10] *Ibid.,* pp. 342–43.

# CHAPTER XII

# Difficulties in Organizing
# and Developing Programs

Pupil personnel services are relatively new, developing rapidly, and characterized by an abundance of energy. Many problems are brought about as a result of difficulties in interpreting these services to other professional and lay people. In some school systems, additional difficulties result from lack of funds. In such instances, the school operates a minimum program of education and is unable to employ specialists in pupil personnel services or, for that matter, in instruction and administration. Some systems have been able to develop only those services in pupil personnel which are required by the state. These are small school systems which dot the nation from east to west and north to south. In them the pupil population often is no more than a few hundred children, and consequently a full program of these services is unjustifiably expensive.

Of the many difficulties which hinder the development of pupil personnel programs, two stand out: (1) difficulties in clarifying and communicating the meaning and business of pupil personnel, and (2) difficulties in training and certification.

### Difficulties in Role Clarification and Communication

The average American citizen observing the activities of the school system is rather clear about the function and general responsibilities of superintendents, principals, and teachers. He is similarly well informed about what goes on in the classroom from kindergarten through senior high school. He knows and understands the work of the athletic coach, the chemistry teacher, the shop teacher, and the elementary school teacher. His contacts with the specialists of the pupil personnel field, however, have been and continue to be limited—so he knows little about the contribution these individuals make to the school program. Certainly, most parents have had very little, if any, contact with the school social worker, the attendance officer, or the school psychologist. They may have become familiar with the school counselor, particularly since Conant's statement about the high school, "There should be one full-time counselor (or guidance officer) for every 250–300 pupils in the high school." [1] And his recommendation for the junior high school: "A full-time specialist, or the equivalent, in guidance and testing should be available for every 250–300 pupils in grades 7 and 8." [2] Also they have heard a great deal about guidance as a result of the National Defense Education Act of 1958, which gives specific support to this aspect of the American school. In general, however, the typical American adult has had very limited direct experience with the field of guidance and with the school counselor.

The lack of parent and community understanding of the work of the various specialists in pupil personnel is a detriment to program development. An even greater handicap in developing these services is the lack of understanding which exists within the school among other members of the professional staff. Many teachers have only a hazy conception of the services performed by some pupil personnel specialists. Others, because of limited contact, have an incorrect impression of the full range of their activities. For example, the teacher who has referred a child to the psychologist will gain a better understanding of the case study phase of his work but may fail in realizing that it is only one of the ways in which he performs.

Generally, the pupil personnel staff is limited in size and consequently is over-burdened with an unfortunately large pupil ratio. They have too many children to see to provide the quality of service they would like to give. Likewise, there are too many teachers to be served in the period of a given day to allow time for getting acquainted with the teacher and helping her get a clearer understanding of the services.

Also complicating this picture is the fact that many of the pupil personnel workers, in addition to being members of the education profession, are members of another profession, such as social work, psychology, or medicine. This fact alone tends to make it difficult

---

[1] James B. Conant, *The American High School Today* (New York: McGraw-Hill Book Company, Inc., 1959), p. 44.

[2] James B. Conant, *A Memorandum to School Boards: Recommendations for Education in the Junior High School Years* (Princeton, N.J.: Educational Testing Service, 1960), p. 27.

for teachers and principals to understand personnel workers and to see clearly how they fit into the school's work. In some states this difficulty is intensified because the educational background and training required of certain of the specialists is limited. The school nurse, for example, is more often than not trained as a public health nurse and has had no specific preparation for employment in the school.[3]

Several states require these specialists to have extensive training in psychology or social work but do not stipulate any need for experiences in education.[4] For example, Connecticut requires at least thirty semester hours of credit from an approved school of social work with supervised social case work experience. Successful teaching experience is allowed as substitute for some of the case work experience but is not specifically required.[5]

All too often the specialist who lacks an educational background fails to understand the work of the teacher and is apt to cause more problems than he helps to correct. Such a school social worker, called by a teacher to help with a child who is demonstrating unadjusted behavior, may suggest a variety of activities which overload the teacher with several new duties: keeping anecdotal material on the child, participating in a parent conference, spending time discussing the case with other specialists, referring back to the child's record and filling out a series of forms, intensifying individual instruction, providing more security, helping the child to participate in social activities. This example, of course, is an exaggeration, but it does illustrate what can occur.

A similar criticism can be leveled against the school psychologist, whose case study reports might make vague recommendations about what needs to be done to correct the child's problems without indicating who is to take responsibility for carrying them out. The recommendations may be difficult, time-consuming, and complicated tasks, such as obtaining a neurological examination, using a kines-

---

[3] Lula P. Dilworth, "Study of Certification of School Nurses by State Departments of Education," *The Journal of School Health,* Vol. XXVIII, No. 3 (1958), 63–78.

[4] Walter L. Hodges, "State Certification of School Psychologists," *The American Psychologist,* 15, No. 6 (1960), 346–49.

[5] *The Team Approach in Pupil Personnel Services,* A Report by the Advisory Pupil Personnel Committee Dealing with the Role of School Social Workers, School Psychologists and School Counselors, Bulletin 69 (Hartford, Conn.: Connecticut State Department of Education, June, 1958), p. 10.

thetic method of teaching reading, or providing isolation for the youngster during certain class periods. The implication is that since the report goes to the principal and the teacher, it is their job to see that these things are carried out. It is indeed questionable whether such recommendations should be passed on to anyone without some specific directions or an offer of help from the psychologist himself.

In some situations, the opposite problem can occur if the specialist has been highly trained and experienced in classroom teaching but has limited training in his area of specialization. In such a case it is difficult for the teachers to perceive that he has anything unique to offer. In Virginia, for example, the school social worker or visiting teacher must have a background of teaching experience preceded by a great deal of pre-service education course work but may have limited social work background. A bulletin of the Virginia State Board of Education states:

> Three years of successful teaching experience, or two years of successful teaching and one year of social work are required for approval for the position of visiting teacher. The adjustment of the child in school and the interpretation of the school program to parents constitute the heart of the visiting teacher's role. Successful teaching experience, therefore, is highly desirable for the greatest effectiveness of the visiting teacher-services.[6]

These people often change from the classroom teaching role to the specialist's role in the same community. They are working with the same teachers who knew them as classroom teachers and who recall clearly their strengths and weaknesses in that role. Often they must overcome these impressions in order to perform adequately in their new job as nonteaching specialists.

Closely related is the difficulty pupil personnel specialists often experience when teachers view with a jaundiced eye any member of the school staff who is a specialist or an "expert." Teachers are inclined to be suspicious of any school staff person who is not faced with many of the same problems that regularly confront them. The personnel worker does not have, in most instances, a class schedule, a homeroom, or lesson plans to prepare. He does not have to contend with many irritations which continuously beset the teacher—

---

[6] *Visiting Teacher in Virginia's Program of Education*, Virginia State Board of Education Bulletin, Vol. XXXVIII, No. 13 (June, 1956), 30–31.

the irate parent complaining of a child's report cards, the overprotective mother sitting in the back of the classroom, and forty children for whom he must not only provide instruction but also by law assume the responsibilities of a parent.

The pupil personnel worker in clarifying his work faces difficulties caused by the rapid and continuous changes in technique and method that are taking place in many areas of school work.. Each year, for example, the number of new group tests available greatly increases. Each time a new test is introduced into the school, the person responsible—often a pupil personnel specialist—must see that it is understood by those who are planning to use it. Similarly, psychologists and other specialists are constantly calling upon teachers to use new forms for referring a child for case study, for keeping anecdotal material on a child with a problem, for identifying children with difficulties, or for a variety of other purposes. Certainly in most instances the reasons for the new forms and procedures are valid for they promise to improve the quality of the educational program. However, in order to be understood, new forms and procedures must be built upon familiar ones. There must not be too much change, and what change there is should be introduced carefully and thoughtfully. The success of pupil personnel services often depends upon the ability of the specialists to help teachers understand and accept changes in techniques and methods without confusion or resentment.

Other difficulties in communication and job clarification occur in attempting to help school administrators understand the pupil personnel function. The background of most administrators as regards the organization and administration of the special programs of pupil personnel, is limited. Specialists in personnel work must assume the responsibility of clarifying for their superiors how their specific competencies are to be used to the advantage of the school program. Communication here is a critical responsibility of all specialists, for unless their superiors understand clearly the services they can perform, it cannot be expected that teachers, parents, and pupils will. Statements of policy, which establish the roles and functions of pupil personnel, are the responsibility of chief administrators working with the staff. In a sense, the pupil personnel worker actually has no function until it is clarified and articulated by his superiors.

These are only some of the difficulties faced in attempting to clarify and interpret the pupil personnel program and the role of the specialists. These difficulties are not entirely unique to pupil personnel, for many other educational workers have similar problems. In instruction and administration new programs are being developed and new specialists are continuously coming into the school program. They too face the necessity of making clear the scope of their new programs and the nature of their ever-changing roles.

## Difficulties in Training and Certification

Difficulties can also occur in the areas of training and certification. Common to virtually all branches of education is the difficulty in obtaining well-prepared, competent workers. It is very much of a problem in pupil personnel services where the need and demand often exceeds the supply.

Trainers of pupil personnel specialists have a particularly difficult task—integration of the area of noneducational professional preparation with that in education. They view with great concern their obligation to train individuals who will be a credit to the profession and at times lose sight of the competencies to be developed if these specialists are to perform adequately in the school setting. In the fields of psychology and social work, however, progress is being made through joint departmental planning. Another area which is changing is the education of school nurses. Many nurses receive their training in hospitals or medical training centers where there is very little tradition of relating the program to the needs of school nursing. In fact, fewer than half of the fifty state departments or boards of education certificate school nurses.[7]

Counselor education presents a different sort of problem. Because of the tremendous increase in student enrollments, training programs have become overburdened. Certification, like training, is lagging. Although noticeable progress has been made recently both in the quality of existing certification patterns and in the development of certificates in states which formerly had none, many states still have not progressed at all.[8]

---

[7] Lula P. Dilworth, op. cit., pp. 63–78.

[8] W. Earl Armstrong and T. M. Stinnett, A Manual on Certification Requirements for School Personnel in the United States (Washington, D.C.: National Education Association, 1959).

Perhaps one of the most difficult and unfortunate training and certification problems occurs in the field of child accounting and attendance—particularly in the training of attendance workers. The simple fact is that there are almost no training programs to prepare specialists for this area of work, and only about a half dozen states provide certification. It is virtually impossible to find anybody who has any particular enthusiasm for developing training programs. It would probably be equally difficult to recruit students to enroll even if programs were available. Present workers in this field, when questioned, usually comment that the only kind of training that will help them is an in-service, on-the-job program. The officers of professional organizations composed of accounting and attendance workers reflect this attitude. Although in-service education is of merit for all specialists in pupil personnel, it is highly desirable that their total preparation include some theory and pre-service training.

These are the difficulties faced by pupil personnel workers in their attempt to improve the quality of their services. The job of the specialist in the schools is a difficult one at best, and is particularly so for pupil personnel workers since they are new in the schools and come with unusual training, different concepts, and new techniques and devices. Yet, if this area of education is to prosper and programs of pupil personnel are to be developed, these difficulties will have to be overcome.

# CHAPTER XIII

# Educational Problems
# Confronting Pupil Personnel

Many broad problems and issues which confront education in America today have a special significance for the field of pupil personnel. The population explosion is creating some particularly difficult problems for specialists in child accounting and attendance and the pupil adjustment services of pupil personnel. Similarly, juvenile delinquency, school drop-outs, and problems resulting from the broadening responsibilities in American elementary and secondary schools have specific meaning and significance for the pupil personnel program.

## Problems of Increasing Pupil Enrollments

In 1900, 15,503,000 children were enrolled in American public elementary and secondary schools. By 1930, this number had increased to 25,678,000.[1] A recent research report of the National Education Association indicates that during the 1960–61 school year 37,244,284 were in attendance.[2] This is a rather phenomenal growth; and according to predictions by population experts, it will continue. Such increases place great strain on the school's programs and facilities and require adaptations in physical plant, teacher personnel, and curriculum. Also, these demands come at a time when vast qualitative changes are being made in the school program. Truly, the American scene in education is an expansive one; it is growing in just about every conceivable dimension, and there are many indications that this growth will continue and lead to even more change.

---

[1] Nelda Umbeck, *State Legislation on School Attendance and Related Matters— School Census and Child Labor,* U.S. Department of Health, Education, and Welfare Circular No. 573 (Washington, D.C.: U.S. Office of Education, January 1, 1959), p. 15.

[2] "School Statistics: 1960–61," *NEA Research Bulletin,* Vol. 39, No. 1 (February, 1961), 3.

Educators during the last several decades have been struggling vigorously to keep ahead of rising school enrollments and the various community and professional pressures which are in a large measure responsible for the new developments in the American schools.

Primarily, the responsibility for anticipating the community's needs in education rests with the board of education and the superintendent of schools. Plans for buildings, equipment, and teachers are often based upon census data provided by pupil personnel. It is thus possible to predict the size of the pupil population to be expected in any school district for almost any projected period of time.

## The Drop-Out Problem

Despite the fact that more children are staying in school longer, the problems of school retention and drop-out still face pupil personnel.

In 1959 the nation's public secondary schools enrolled 72.8 per cent of all youth in the 14–17 age group, as compared with 24 per cent after World War I and 10 per cent at the turn of the century. As impressive as the gain is, the number of students who leave school before graduation, particularly the 16- and 17-year-olds, is alarming. A United States Office of Education study shows, ". . . only about 60 per cent of those who were in the fifth grade 7 years before actually graduate from high school each year." [3]

A similar study reported by the National Education Association commented on the number of school years completed by persons who have come through the American elementary and secondary school program. Fifteen states show medians of 10 or more years of schooling completed for persons over 25 years of age. Utah led the nation with 12 years. The lowest ranking states were Louisiana and South Carolina with 7.6 each; Georgia with 7.8; and Alabama and North Carolina with 7.9 each. The national median was reported as 9.3. [4]

[3] Edmund A. Ford and Virgil R. Walker, *Public Secondary Schools: Statistics of Education in the United States, 1958–59 Series* (No. 1), U.S. Department of Health, Education, and Welfare (Washington, D.C.: Government Printing Office, 1961), p. 5.

[4] *Rankings of the States,* NEA Research Division (Washington, D.C.: National Education Association, January, 1957), p. 4.

These and similar studies reveal that the drop-out rate is still very high and a constant source of irritation to the school and community. Many of the children who drop out are the ones who most urgently need the benefits of the school programs for, with technical advances occurring at a rapid pace, manpower needs require the development of a high degree of technical competency among persons entering the labor market. The demand for semi-skilled and unskilled workers is diminishing each year. Much of the responsibility for providing vocational competence rests on the elementary and secondary schools. The schools in general and pupil personnel in particular must be concerned about the drop-out problem and also with the large number of youngsters who should be going on to higher education but who are stopping at high school graduation.

### The Problem of Juvenile Delinquency

Schools in Europe and America have long been concerned with problems of juvenile delinquency. One of the primary motives underlying early compulsory educational legislation was to keep children off the street. This motive was reflected in early laws which stated that it was the school's responsibility to teach children to be informed about and to respect the laws of the land.

The school is perhaps the most important of all of the community's institutions in the prevention and control of the problem of juvenile delinquency. This is pointed out by McClusky, who discusses the role of several community agencies in a recent yearbook of the National Society for the Study of Education:

> It should be clear by this time that the school is only one of the community's many resources for the protection of youth. But it should be equally clear that the school occupies a uniquely favorable position, some would say the most favorable, for seeing that the total resources of the community are mobilized. It is present in every community. It has all the children of all the people. Of all agencies it has the largest equipment, property, and staff. While second in influence to the home, it has, through the children, the most universal and practical access to parents.[5]

---

[5] Howard Y. McClusky, "How Community Agencies May Help With Problems of Delinquency," *Juvenile Delinquency and the Schools,* Forty-Seventh Yearbook of the National Society for the Study of Education, Part I, ed. Nelson B. Henry (Chicago: The University of Chicago Press, 1948), p. 212.

The incidence of crime among school-age children in some measure is an index of the effectiveness of the school in dealing with youth's needs and problems. Again quoting the Yearbook,

> In a way, therefore, a yearbook on delinquency is an admission of failure—failure in the nation as well as in the schools. The juvenile-delinquency rate is an index of the social, emotional, and moral maladjustment of a nation.[6]

The school's concern with juvenile delinquency involves every phase of the school's program. Perhaps most important are the responsibilities which fall within the pupil personnel department. The Yearbook indicates this importance by devoting specific attention to the part played by pupil personnel services in the prevention of juvenile delinquency.

Further evidence is found in the many specific job responsibilities assigned to pupil personnel specialists in local programs which relate directly to this problem. Following is a list of some of those duties which were abstracted from descriptions of pupil personnel programs in 35 Ohio school districts:

1. Visit the homes of truant pupils and issue warnings.
2. Represent the school in court in cases of juvenile offense.
3. Assist in handling of problems of discipline.
4. Investigate cases where pupils are not attending school regularly.
5. Supply social history information to the courts, police departments, or social agencies when requested in connection with a school child.
6. Prevent serious problems through a program of early identification.
7. Study and treat all cases which might eventuate in acts of delinquency.[7]

Voorhees, studying pupil personnel activities in selected school districts, found liaison work with juvenile court and/or welfare agents to be a specific responsibility in 96.7 per cent of the 82 districts investigated. Of eighteen specific responsibilities which were investigated in this study, only one, liaison with the home, was more frequently cited as a specific pupil personnel duty.[8]

---

[6] *Ibid.*, p. 8.

[7] Taken from an unpublished study conducted by the author.

[8] Leonard B. Voorhees, "A Descriptive Study of the Organization, Administration, and Operation of Pupil Personnel Services in Selected School Districts" (Doctoral dissertation presented at Michigan State University, 1960), pp. 95–96.

Numerous studies of the characteristics of juvenile delinquents reveal a large number of significant symptoms which occur in the school. Kvaraceus, in the *Encyclopedia of Educational Research,* summarizes several of these studies and points to the deviations in the behavior of delinquent children which relate directly to school activities:

*Deviations in School*

"Poor" or failure marks
Repeater (retarded in grade)
Strong dislike and hostility for school
Truancy
Intent to leave school early
Vague or no educational-vocational goals
Motivational problem
Member of special class
Has attended many different schools
Destroys school material and property
Does not feel he "belongs" in classroom
Does not participate in volunteer extracurricular school activities
Seriously and persistently misbehaving in school[9]

It can be clearly seen that each of these deviations is of direct concern to one or several of the specialists in pupil personnel.

## Problems of Expanding School Responsibilities

American elementary and secondary schools have received a great deal of attention in recent years which focuses in part on the tremendous expansion which has occurred in the school's responsibilities. Much of this attention has taken the form of negative criticism. Not only do the critics indict the schools for assuming responsibilities that they claim are more appropriately those of parents and the home and other community agencies, but they also reprimand the schools for not adequately doing the job for which they are primarily intended. A cogent judgment in this regard is that of John H. Fischer, President and former Dean of Teachers College, Columbia University. Dr. Fischer states:

The school's traditional responsibility for systematically instructing children in the cultural heritage and developing their intellectual

9 William C. Kvaraceus, "Delinquency," *Encyclopedia of Educational Research,* 3rd ed. (New York: The Macmillan Company, 1960), p. 367.

competence has received relatively less attention than some of the newer items on the educational agenda. Not only has the school been asked to offer more kinds of instruction for pupils; it is expected also to be a center for entertainment, civic development, charitable enterprises, and other more or less good works which, although they are conducted under the school's roof and in its stadium, can hardly be called educational. In addition, schools have been assigned or have assumed more and more responsibility in such fields as medicine, social case work, and clinical psychology.[10]

Certainly the school is constantly under community pressure to provide new or extended services. The curriculum is being continuously broadened to include new programs of instruction, such as honors and advanced placement sections in mathematics, science, English, and foreign language; and new programs in life adjustment education. Also, many elementary and secondary school programs are being lengthened to include kindergarten and junior college, respectively.

Several of the newer programs relate directly to the pupil personnel function, particularly those which are often described as clinical services—medical, dental, psychological, social work. It is the obligation of the school's responsible officials to weigh and measure the validity of such suggestions and decide whether they represent an intrusion upon the real function of the school.

It is not within the scope of this book to judge whether these services are more appropriately school or community responsibilities. It is desirable, however, to point out that many of these services are performed by individuals who have been specifically trained to work in the school setting with problems that have a direct bearing on the effectiveness with which the school achieves its aims. On the other hand, it is equally necessary to point out that there are functions of medicine, psychology, and social work which have no direct bearing on the school's responsibilities in the community and therefore are more properly assigned to community or private agencies.

The line dividing the school's role from the community's is not at all clear and opinions differ. Certainly an issue exists which warrants careful consideration, for the pressures to move in the direction of broader school services are strong. Each of the problems and issues discussed in this chapter will require the continuing at-

---

[10] John H. Fischer, "Schools are for Learning," *Saturday Review, Education Supplement,* Vol. XLIII, No. 38 (September 17, 1960), 72.

tention of all professional educators. These, only a few of many, were selected because of their special pertinence to pupil personnel services.

Pupil personnel services must be viewed within the total school program. They involve consideration of educational objectives, administrative jobs, teachers' roles, and specialists who contribute unique services to all of education.

Pupil personnel is a group of services and functions in elementary and secondary schools which aim to adapt the school program to the needs of the learner and to adjust the learner to the school program. It involves locating the children who should be in school, seeing that they get to school, and keeping them there under conditions that will permit them to profit from the school experience. It serves pupils and teachers through (1) records—cumulative, anecdotal, and case study; (2) psychological studies; (3) psychiatric services; (4) counseling; (5) field services; (6) follow-up services; (7) special adaptive programs for those who must be given extra help to attend regularly or to profit from school; (8) health services; and (9) child accounting and attendance services. The aims of pupil personnel are those of all American education: providing for the intellectual, physical, emotional, and social development of all pupils.

Historically, pupil personnel involves four periods of development. The first period includes the passing of compulsory education laws; the second, the passing of compulsory attendance laws. The third period—beginning with the first decade of the twentieth century—emphasized studies to prevent attendance difficulties, and marked the appearance of guidance, school psychology, the visiting teacher, the school nurse, group testing and the child-centered philosophy of education. The present period is characterized by the appearance of additional services and a trend toward the coordination of pupil personnel services in the local school and on the state level.

# Bibliography

American Psychological Association, *The Psychologist on the School Staff*, Report of the Committee on Reconsideration of the Functions of the School Psychologist. Washington, D.C.: American Psychological Association, Division 16, October, 1958.

Arbuckle, Dugald S., *Pupil Personnel Services in American Schools*. Boston: Allyn & Bacon, Inc., 1962.

Bower, Eli Michael, *The School Psychologist*, California State Department of Education Bulletin, Vol. XXIV, No. 12. Sacramento, Calif., 1955.

California State Department of Education, *The Preparation and Training of Pupil Personnel Workers*, Report of the State Committee on Credentials for Pupil Personnel Services, Vol. XXI, No. 5. Sacramento, Calif., 1952.

Connecticut State Department of Education, *The Team Approach in Pupil Personnel Services*, A Report by the Advisory Pupil Personnel Committee Dealing with the Role of School Social Workers, School Psychologists, and School Counselors, Bulletin 69. Hartford, Conn., 1958.

Cook, Katherine M., *The Place of Visiting Teacher Services in the School Program*, Federal Security Agency Bulletin 1945, No. 6. Washington, D.C.: U.S. Government Printing Office, 1945.

Council of Chief State School Officers, *Responsibility of State Departments of Education for Pupil Personnel Services: A Policy Statement*. Washington, D.C.: Counsel of Chief State School Officers, 1960.

Cutts, Norma E., ed., *School Psychologists at Mid-Century*. Washington, D.C.: American Psychological Association, Inc., 1955.

Davis, Frank G., ed., *Pupil Personnel Service*. Scranton, Pa.: The International Textbook Company, 1948.

Fusco, Gene C., *Organization and Administration of Pupil Personnel Service Programs in Selected School Systems*. Washington, D.C.: U.S. Department of Health, Education, and Welfare, 1961.

Gottsegen, Monroe G., and Gloria B. Gottsegen, ed., *Professional School Psychology*. New York: Grune and Stratton, 1960.

Hatch, Raymond N. and Buford Stefflre, *Administration of Guidance Services: Organization, Supervision, Evaluation*. Englewood Cliffs, N.J.: Prentice-Hall, Inc., 1958.

Heck, Arch O., *Administration of Pupil Personnel*. Boston: Ginn and Company, 1929.

Henry, Nelson B., ed., *Juvenile Delinquency and the Schools*, The Forty-Seventh Yearbook of the National Society for the Study of Education, Part II. Chicago: The University of Chicago Press, 1948.

————, ed., *Personnel Services in Education*, The Fifty-Eighth Yearbook of the National Society for the Study of Education, Part II. Chicago: The University of Chicago Press, 1959.

Hutson, Percival W., *The Guidance Function in Education.* New York: Appleton-Century-Crofts, Inc., 1958.

Johnson, Walter T., Buford Stefflre, and Roy A. Edelfelt, *Pupil Personnel and Guidance Services.* New York: McGraw-Hill Book Company, Inc., 1961.

Johnston, Edgar G., Mildred Peters, and William Evraiff, *The Role of the Teacher in Guidance.* Englewood Cliffs, N.J.: Prentice-Hall, Inc., 1959.

Mathewson, Robert H., *Guidance Policy and Practice.* New York: Harper & Row, Publishers, 1949.

McCormick, John, ed., *Exceptional Children.* Washington, D.C.: The Council for Exceptional Children, Department of the NEA.

Nemir, Alma, *The School Health Program.* Philadelphia: W. B. Saunders Company, 1959.

Oberteuffer, Delbert, ed., *The Journal of School Health.* Kent, Ohio: The American School Health Association.

"Pupil Personnel, Guidance, and Counseling," *Review of Educational Research,* III:3 (June, 1933); XXI:2 (April, 1951); XXIV:1 (February, 1954); XXIV:2 (April, 1954). Washington, D.C.: American Educational Research Association.

Reed, Anna Y., *Guidance and Personnel Services in Education,* 3rd ed. Ithaca, N.Y.: Cornell University Press, 1947.

Rosecrance, Francis C. and Velma D. Hayden, *School Guidance and Personnel Services.* Boston: Allyn & Bacon, Inc., 1960.

Roser, Mark, ed., *International Association of Pupil Personnel Workers Journal.* Allentown, Pa.: International Association of Pupil Personnel Workers.

Samler, Joseph, ed., *The Personnel and Guidance Journal.* Washington, D.C.: American Personnel and Guidance Association, Inc., 1961.

Stoops, Emery, ed., *Guidance Services: Organization and Administration.* New York: McGraw-Hill Book Company, Inc., 1959.

Strang, Ruth, *Pupil Personnel and Guidance.* New York: The Macmillan Company, 1941.

Umbeck, Nelda, *State Legislation on School Attendance and Related Matters—School Census and Child Labor,* U.S. Department of Health, Education, and Welfare Circular No. 573. Washington, D.C., January 1, 1959.

Voorhees, Leonard B., "A Descriptive Study of the Organization, Administration, and Operation of Pupil Personnel Services in Selected School Districts." Unpublished doctoral dissertation presented at Michigan State University, 1960.

Willey, Roy DeVerl, *Guidance in Elementary Education.* New York: Harper & Row, Publishers, 1952.

Wilson, Charles C., ed., *School Health Services.* Washington, D.C.: National Education Association, 1953.

Wrenn, C. Gilbert, *The Counselor in A Changing World.* Washington, D.C.: American Personnel and Guidance Association, 1962.

Yeager, William A., *Administration and the Pupil.* New York: Harper & Row, Publishers, 1949.

# Index

### A

Administration of pupil personnel services, 3, 31-37, 47
administrative specialist, director, 34, 35-37
training and certification, 36-37
criticisms of administrative patterns, 34-35
departmentalization, 31-35
Alabama, 102
American Association of School Administrators, 83
American Medical Association, 18, 80, 83
American Personnel and Guidance Association, 21, 47
American Psychological Association, 21, 51-52, 55-56, 58
American Psychological Association, Division, 16, 21
American School Health Association, 79, 83
Armstrong, W. Earl, 67
Army General Classification Test, 19
Arnold, Dwight L., 41
Association for Supervision and Curriculum Development, 49
Attendance (*see* Child accounting and attendance)
Attendance officers:
counseling function, 73
duties, 6, 73-74
police power, 73-74
training and certification, 61, 74-75
Attitudes, detrimental:
of administrators toward pupil personnel programs, 2-3, 23, 26, 95
of parents toward pupil personnel, 2, 93-94
of personnel specialists toward teachers, 95
of teachers toward pupil personnel, 3, 94, 96-97
of the community toward pupil personnel, 94
Audiology, 90 (*see also* Hearing handicapped)

### B

Baltimore, 33
Binet Intelligence Scale, Stanford revision, 19
Binet-Simon test, revised, 19
Blind (*see* Visually handicapped)
B'nai B'rith, 14
Boston, 17, 18
Byrd, Oliver E., 82

### C

California, 21, 48, 51, 59, 62-63
Catholic Social Services, 66
Catholic Youth Organization, 14
Certification (*see* Training and certification)
Chicago, 17, 20, 33
Child accounting and attendance, 8, 24-25, 69-75, 107 (*see also* Attendance officers):
attendance work, 72-75
child accounting, 70-72
child accounting and attendance work distinguished, 69
functions, 6, 8, 69, 72-73
history, 16-17, 69
*Choosing a Vocation,* by F. Parsons, 17
Cincinnati, 18
Cleveland, 18, 33
Columbia University, 21
Commonwealth Fund of New York, 20
Communicable disease control, 18-19, 77
and community health, 78
in school health program, 77, 78, 79, 80, 83
Community agencies cooperating with pupil personnel, 14, 18, 66-67
Compulsory education laws, 16
Compulsory school attendance laws, 16, 69, 72, 73-74, 103 (*see also* Dismissal laws):
source of the pupil personnel program, 16
Conant, James B., 94